Dear Sherry,

Thank for your great efforts!

Blessing & Shalom!

PEACE FOR PEACE

ISRAEL IN THE NEW MIDDLE EAST

DAVID RUBIN

Shiloh
ISRAEL*Press*

Peace For Peace:
Israel in the New Middle East

ISBN: 978-0-9829067-4-3

Published by Shiloh Israel Press

Contact The Author
david@ShilohIsraelChildren.org

Contact The Publisher
sipress@ShilohIsraelChildren.org

For Orders:
1-800-431-1579 (toll-free)

Book Production
Prestige Prepress
prestige.prepress@gmail.com

Cover Design and Layout
Christopher Tobias

Printed in Israel

This book is dedicated in memory of the nearly 1,600 Israelis who have been killed by Islamic terrorists from the signing of the Oslo Accords peace agreement in September of 1993 until the end of 2012. That is an enormous number in a country smaller in size than New Jersey.

They were coldly labeled as "sacrifices for peace" by many of Israel's misguided politicians, including some of the top echelon. The tragic national scandal is that their lives were snuffed out in exchange for nothing. No peace was given in return and the past twenty years have seen the greatest frequency of terrorism and war in modern Israel's history.

Most of the names of the victims will be forgotten and the suffering of their family members won't be discussed anymore on the evening news, nor will the suffering of the thousands of Israelis who have been wounded in these past twenty years.

Even so, the mainstream media will continue to promote (Israeli) land for (promises of) peace, as the centerpiece of a misguided peace process that is going nowhere. My hope is that this book will change some misconceived notions of how to achieve peace for Israel in a hostile Middle East environment that is increasingly in turmoil.

As for those 1,600 victims whose lives were abruptly cut short, we will remember and try to learn the lessons that they have unintentionally bequeathed to us.

May their memory be a blessing for all of those who loved them, as well as for the entire people of Israel in the ongoing struggle for survival.

Contents

About The Author

David Rubin is a former mayor of Shiloh, Israel – in the region of Samaria, known to much of the world as the West Bank. He is the founder and president of Shiloh Israel Children's Fund (SICF) – dedicated to healing the trauma of children who have been victims of terrorist attacks, as well as rebuilding the biblical heartland of Israel. SICF was established after Rubin and his three-year-old son were wounded in a vicious terrorist attack while driving home from Jerusalem. Rubin vowed to retaliate – not with hatred, nor with anger, but with compassion – in order to affect positive change for Israel and its children.

Rubin's first book was *God, Israel, and Shiloh: Returning to the Land,* which tells the story of the very human struggles and triumphs of Israel's complex history, dating back to slavery in Egypt and continuing up to the present. Rubin describes Israel's miraculous return to its biblical heartland, and the subsequent challenge of its residents to rebuild, despite the constant threat of terrorism and the trauma of the many terrorist attacks that have affected their communities. Rubin's second book was the groundbreaking *The Islamic Tsunami: Israel and America in the Age of Obama,* which boldly exposes the danger to Israel, America and Judeo-Christian civilization posed by the Islamic ideologues and their odd collusion with the far secular Left. Both of these books are as relevant today as when they were first published.

A featured speaker throughout North America, Europe, and in Israel, David Rubin is a frequent guest commentator on national and international radio and television programs.

Born and raised in Brooklyn, NY, Rubin resides in Israel with his wife and children on a hilltop overlooking the site of Ancient Shiloh. This is the hallowed ground where the Tabernacle of Israel stood for 369 years in the time of Joshua, Hannah, and Samuel the Prophet.

Introduction

On the eve of Israel's national elections in 1996, with peace process icon Shimon Peres the odds-on favorite to be elected as Prime Minister, Israel was rocked by a sudden string of terrorist attacks, including bus bombings, with a great number of fatalities and many more wounded. It was a shocking reminder that the new Middle East of peace and cooperation that Peres had proclaimed with such glowing optimism had perhaps not yet arrived. Two decades later, Israelis are more skeptical than ever – with fewer and fewer believing that peace is on the horizon. Not only has the peace process fallen flat on its face, but events and trends in the Middle East are spinning at a breathtaking speed. The revolution in Egypt, the civil war in Syria, the war in Gaza, the Iranian nuclear threat and conflict – all of these potentially explosive developments are rapidly changing the Middle East – shaking it to the core – and the ramifications for Israel should not be underestimated.

I remember a conversation I had with a friend of mine here in Israel back in 1996, shortly after the reports came in about yet another bus bombing in Jerusalem. I pointed out my perception that almost every day in those few months, there had either been another terrorist attack, or a new bold headline of political intrigue, or another abrupt strange twist in the tumultuous peace process. I told him that it seemed to have been an extremely eventful year with no respite for those folks who like peace and quiet in their lives. His quick response was that in Israel, there is never a dull year nor is there ever a dull moment. That doesn't mean that one can't have peace of mind in Israel, but in my twenty plus years living in Israel, I have never ceased to be amazed at the next turn of events that always seems to be waiting around the corner.

Many of the events, the changes, and the political spin are directly related to, or are a product of the vaunted peace process, the seemingly intractable and complicated quest for an elusive end to the war, the terrorism, and the suffering that afflicts the Middle East. It has become a given in Israeli politics, American politics, and world politics in general, that there always has to be a peace process in the Middle East. Just as the sun has to shine and the Earth has to revolve around it, there has to be a peace process. Every few years, a new peace plan is bandied about and the politicians loudly declare that the time is ripe for peace. It doesn't matter that each newly promoted peace plan is based on formulas that haven't worked in the past. Just as every serious college professor has to come out with a new research article periodically, the politician that wants his foreign relations credentials to be taken seriously has to be promoting a peace plan. The Russians, the French, the British, and even the United Nations, with its endless flow of anti-Israel resolutions – all desire to be "a player" in the strange game known as the peace process.

One could easily fill a room with the books that have been written about the peace process, mostly by Israeli and American politicians. Obviously it sells, especially if the author is a former president, prime minister, foreign minister, secretary of state, or a defense minister and it gives the author an added credibility as he moves on to his next challenge in life. That's all well and good, but the problem lies in the result. Is it just interesting reading, or are we truly learning how to achieve a lasting peace in this part of the world? With each book about the peace process, are we in fact getting closer to resolving the conflict?

Unfortunately, I have to answer with a resounding "No".

After billions of dollars spent by governments, particularly the United States, and thousands of hours expended by foreign policy experts and political leaders, the quest for peace in the Middle East has been an utter failure, but we continue to play the game according to the same rules. For example, we still relate to the United Nations as a legitimate player in the process, even though it has become a cesspool of hatred for Israel. I might add that if the United States wasn't far and away its largest funder, the international body would be more open about its hatred of the United States, as well.

In the past few years, Israel has seen three major military conflicts bordering on war, once with the Hezbollah terrorist organization in Lebanon and twice with the Gaza-based Hamas. In each of these conflicts, we have stopped short of achieving clear-cut victory after intense international pressure to agree to premature ceasefires.

I am often asked, "Has Israel lost the will to survive?" It is indeed a legitimate question. With well over 100,000 missiles being pointed at our cities and towns and with countless bomb factories and weapons-smuggling tunnels threatening our daily existence, our political leadership often suffers from neck cramps from the constant looking over their shoulders, deeply anxious about world opinion. Despite the fact that Zionism is the movement of Jewish independence, Israelis remain hyper-sensitive about what the assorted world leaders will say if Israel decides to take the initiative and takes preemptive action, with the understanding that the best defense is a good offense. Are we so obsessed with what the other nations will say and how it might damage the stagnant peace process that we have lost the ability to act in our own self-interests?

Peace for Peace: Israel In The New Middle East is a response to the paralysis in both thinking and action that has frustrated the search for a lasting peace in the Middle East between Israel and its Islamic neighbors. This book examines the meaning of peace and why, despite all of the good intentions, it has been so difficult to achieve. We review the full history of the conflict and the various attempts at resolution – the summits, the peace plans, and the literary attempts at explaining both. The ongoing and growing culture clash with the Islamic world and the earth-shaking events of the Arab Spring are analyzed in this context, as the ramifications for peace with Israel are significant and cannot be ignored. We then zero in on the key issues of dispute that have stymied the attempts at reaching a regional peace. We examine the facts, while simultaneously disposing of the myths and the mantras that have prevented progress up to this point in time.

Finally, I present Peace for Peace, my comprehensive plan for peace between Israel and its neighbors, a common sense plan with eyes open, a plan that doesn't ignore the religious-cultural conflict, a plan that is biblically and historically based. Most importantly, it is a Zionist plan in which Israel takes its destiny into its own hands. Peace for Peace can bring a lasting peace for Israel in the midst of an increasingly volatile and potentially hostile new Middle East.

PEACE
FOR
PEACE

ISRAEL IN
THE NEW
MIDDLE EAST

CHAPTER ONE

The Thirst For Peace

Imagine all the people living life in peace ...[1]

(John Lennon)

Peace is that brief glorious moment in history when everybody stands around reloading.[2]

(Thomas Jefferson)

The road to peace will always be strewn with risks, but I prefer the risks of peace over the agonies of war.[3]

(Israeli Prime Minister Ehud Olmert, October 2007)

Peace. Shalom. While certainly a universal concept desired by most people, the quest for peace and the struggle for peace has always typified Israelis and Jews, a people who have never known much peace. I think it can be fairly stated that no people has spoken about peace so often, written about it so extensively, but has experienced so little of it from its enemies. Israel's intense thirst for peace, coupled with the Jewish state's lack of it, is indeed one of the great paradoxes of modern times.

Peace is, at its core, an essentially biblical concept, deeply rooted in the ancient religious texts of Israel. The word "Shalom" is found 376 times in the Torah, or the Tanach – the complete Jewish Bible – known to most of the world as The Old Testament.[4] In Hebrew, the ancient language of the Torah, every letter has a numerical equivalent (known as Gematria), often denoting deep spiritual meanings, while at other times, the meanings are not so clear, but the numerical amounts and patterns are often so logical and so in sync with current events, that it's hard to believe that they are purely coincidental. Shalom is a case in point, mentioned 376 times, and when you add up the numerical amounts of the letters, you have a sum of 376, revealing the significance of peace as a central concept in Judaism. The word is used in many different contexts, with a variety of meanings. However, the sheer number of times that the word appears in the Bible makes it abundantly clear to all that peace is a central biblical and universal value that all nations are advised to pursue, but specifically the nation of Israel, who presented the Torah's lofty concepts to the entire world.

Turn from evil and do good, seek peace and pursue it.
(Psalms 34:15)

The beautiful Psalms that were composed by King David some 3,000 years ago reverberate to this day in their poetic eloquence and praise of peace. However, David was not some card-carrying member of the extreme Peace Now movement, nor was he a charismatic speaker at avowedly non-violent anti-war rallies. On the contrary, King David was well known as a celebrated warrior and conqueror of enemy nations. Of King David, it is said that, despite his greatness, he was not permitted to build the Holy Temple in Jerusalem because his hands were stained with blood from his many battles.

He summoned his son Solomon and commanded him to build a Temple for the Lord, God of Israel. David said to Solomon, "My son, I had in mind to build a Temple for the Name of the Lord my God, but the word of the Lord came to me saying, 'You have shed much blood and have made great wars; you shall not build a Temple for My Name's sake, for you have shed much blood upon the ground before Me.'"

(Chronicles 22:6-8)

Even though David's many battles were considered to be righteous and necessary wars to possess and defend the

Land of Israel, the task and privilege of building God's Holy Temple in Jerusalem was passed along to his son and successor to the throne, the wise King Solomon. The blood from wars was simply incompatible with the peace and sanctity of the Holy Temple.[5]

Since Israel was reestablished as an independent, sovereign nation in 1948, the land of Israel has been bombarded with a nearly ceaseless torrent of wars and terrorism to a disproportionate degree never before experienced in human civilization. Surrounded by enemy nations, assaulted by terrorist organizations from the north, from the south, and

A Necessary Battle, But Incompatible With The Peace Of The Temple: *Little David stands up to the giant Philistine, Goliath. He was a great warrior, but wasn't chosen to build the Temple.*

from within, Israel's political leadership nonetheless has always been obsessed with the search for peace. It didn't matter that the Arab nations surrounding Israel were perpetually threatening to "drive the Jews into the sea" both before and after each war, in which those stubborn Jews always somehow emerged victorious. Even so, Israel's political leadership has always expressed its willingness to withdraw from conquered lands in exchange for genuine promises of peace or, until recently, the absence of war. In modern history, it is almost unheard of for the winning nation to surrender land that it has rightfully taken

The Unified Kingdom Of Biblical Israel

Two Banks Of The Jordan River: *David's Unified Kingdom included both sides of the Jordan River – the West Bank and the East Bank.*

possession of in a defensive war. Indeed, it is rare for the victor to do anything other than to dictate the terms of the truce and/ or peaceful resolution to the conflict.

> *To the victors go the spoils.*[6]
> (US Senator William Marcy, 1831)

After 2000 years of exile from the Land of Israel, after 2000 years of dispersion and persecution, after 2000 years of expulsions, forced conversions and genocide, the reestablished Israel, in its search for peace and perhaps acceptance into the family of nations, has allowed a change in the rules of the game. The often-discussed peace process between Israel and its neighbors is usually more accurately called a "piece process", a discussion centering on the question of which pieces of land, and how much of it, Israel will surrender in exchange for vague promises of peace. In the United Nations and in other international forums, Israel is the only country that is repeatedly told to give up vital national assets, not to mention its historic capital city, and all in the name of peace. It is frequently accused of being an "obstacle to peace" and "not wanting peace," due to the occasional refusal on the part of some of its leaders to hand over the Jewish nation's sovereignty over its cities and towns to nations and terrorist organizations that are sworn to its destruction. Israel is also called the same names for fighting back after rocket attacks on Israeli cities and towns and after terrorist shooting attacks on Israeli civilians. It is the only country in the world that is expected to allow such attacks without response.

> *Well, the neighborhood bully, he's just one man*
> *His enemies say he's on their land*
> *They got him outnumbered about a million to one*
> *He got no place to escape to, no place to run*
> *He's the neighborhood bully.*
>
> *The neighborhood bully just lives to survive*
> *He's criticized and condemned for being alive*

He's not supposed to fight back
He's supposed to have thick skin
He's supposed to lay down and die
When his door is kicked in
He's the neighborhood bully[7]
(Bob Dylan, "Neighborhood Bully", 1983)

The Size Of Israel
In Comparison To Her Neighbors

Country	Land Mass In Square Miles	Number Of Times Israel Could Fit Into This Country
Israel	8,367	
Lebanon	4,015	0
Jordan	35,637	4
Syria	71,498	9
Iraq	168,754	20
Turkey	301,383	36
Egypt	384,343	46
Iran	636,296	76
Saudi Arabia	756,985	90

A Sense Of Perspective: *Viewing the entire Middle East, one sees the absurdity of demanding Israeli surrender of land.*

If Israel as a whole were to reject out of hand this strange and skewed system of international abuse, it would certainly be reasonable and it would garner no little amount of respect if not love, but sadly, that is not the case. Israel has legitimized the demands by negotiating the surrender of Israel's heartland communities and even its capital city, as if it's an intricate jigsaw puzzle game in which each piece has no intrinsic value. It has accepted as a basic premise that tiny Israel, and only tiny Israel, is the one that needs to surrender land as part of any potential peace agreement. Furthermore, Israel has implicitly agreed to accept terrorist attacks, often with little or no response. This has created dangerous precedence and greatly decreased Israel's power of deterrence.

Under this strangely unbalanced system of international relations in the rules of war and diplomacy, the many Arab nations, with their huge land mass some 500 times the land mass of Israel, those same nations who badly lost their war of aggression in 1967, are under no obligation to surrender even an inch of the lands that they control. However, little Israel, the country that won those territories fair and square in a defensive war, is expected to return what it recaptured in the war. We can complain about the inherent lack of fairness in this arrangement that is imposed on us by outside parties, but we can't expect to alter the lack of fairness in the arrangement if the political leadership of Israel has accepted its legitimacy.

As Israel's first prime minister, David Ben-Gurion would often say:

> *"It doesn't matter what the goyim (non-Jews) say. What matters is what the Jews do."*[8]

In other words, we can't expect the non-Jewish world to change the unfair status quo and to be supportive of Israel, if we ourselves don't have the fortitude to fight against an unfair and unjust treatment that ties our hands and prevents us from asserting our national destiny.

We are tired of fighting. We are tired of being courageous. We are tired of winning. We are tired of defeating our enemies.[9]
(Deputy Prime Minister Ehud Olmert, June 2005)

Tired Of Fighting: *Ehud Olmert's statement represented a weakness of spirit that has afflicted many Israelis, for whom the yearning for peace has blinded their resolve.*

These defeatist words, spoken by a man who would soon become the next prime minister of Israel, reflected a serious spiritual malaise that is widespread in some segments of the Israeli population. That yearning for peace in Israel is so strong all across the political spectrum, but when it's derived from tiredness or a lack of belief in the justice of our cause, it can lead to illogical decisions in the pursuit of that peace.

What leads to this tiredness, this malaise, this willingness to surrender to the constant onslaught of bullying and abusive behavior from Israel's enemies and even some ostensibly friendly nations? How is it possible that the embattled nation of Israel, having suffered from centuries of persecution both in its dispersion and in its rebirth, and having survived against all odds, is willing to create a terrorist state in its own biblical heartland, and even in its capital city?

In my vision of peace, there are two free peoples living side by side in this small land, with good neighborly relations and mutual respect, each with its flag, anthem and government, with neither one threatening its neighbor's security and existence.[10]
(Prime Minister Benjamin Netanyahu, June 2009)

Two States Side By Side: *Prime Minister Benjamin Netanyahu endorses the two-state solution in a policy speech at Bar Ilan University, but continues to insist that the Palestinians recognize Israel as the Jewish State.*

In that speech given at Bar Ilan University, Netanyahu expressed his support for the vaunted two-state solution of further dividing the land of Israel into a Jewish state (Israel) and an Arab Muslim state (Palestine). The so-called Palestinian people living in the Land of Israel are represented by three major terrorist organizations. Does Israel's leader truly believe that an agreement with them can lead to peace? Could it be that Israel, as a much maligned and long persecuted and abused nation is suffering from the psychological effects of that abuse?

Countless studies have been carried out analyzing the effects of constant abuse and ongoing harassment on its victims. Most of the research has explored the trauma of the individual victims of sexual and/or physical abuse and the destruction of their self-esteem, often to the extent that they start blaming themselves for the abuse that has been inflicted on them. This unintentional abandonment of the most basic instinct of self-preservation in abuse victims goes a long way to explaining Israel's disproportionate willingness to risk national suicide in exchange for vague promises of peace.

Dr. Kenneth Levin, an instructor of Clinical Psychiatry at Harvard Medical School and a Princeton-trained historian, has referred to the behavior of large segments of the Israeli population as "delusional" and compared such behavior to that of abused children:

> *Abused children always blame themselves for the abuse because they want to believe that they can have control over a situation that is really beyond their control.*

> *The hope is that if they just accept the indictment, if they just repress the recognition that they are being attacked unfairly, and try to change accordingly that somehow they'll win relief from their attackers.*[11]

Taking the research to the level of national victimhood, Levin maintains that the Palestinian Authority (PA), considered to be a realistic partner for peace, was an entirely fictional entity, created by an Israeli government that was desperate to put an end to suffering:

> *They created a partner that didn't exist. They created this image of the other side that was prepared to give them peace in response/exchange for Israeli withdrawals. But that partner did not exist; it was a figment of the imagination.*[12]

It is indeed a fact that the aggrieved wanna-be nation that the entire world now knows as "Palestinians" did not exist until they were created just a few decades ago. While it seem a bit far-fetched that they were actually created by the Israelis (as opposed to the Arabs) because of the abused child syndrome described above, it does go a long way to explaining why successive Israeli governments have been active partners in perpetuating this myth, despite knowing the falsified reading of history on which the existence of this "people" is based.

So what are the facts? Where did the name come from? In the year 63 CE (Current Era), the Romans rulers drove the Jews from their formerly sovereign Land of Israel. At that time, the land, no longer the unified Kingdom of Israel was divided into two parts. The northern region was known as Israel, while the southern region was known as Judea. The Romans did away with both of those names and renamed the entire country "Palestina", a Roman derivative of the term "Philistines", which referred to the nation that was the arch-enemy of Israel, the folks that brought us the infamous Goliath. The Romans understood the power of semantics and sought to linguistically erase the biblical, historical names of Israel in one fell swoop. What better way could there be to wipe Israel off the map than to change the name of its homeland, where its citizens had dwelled as a sovereign people for nearly a thousand years and in a semi-sovereign status for several hundred more?

In truth, the Roman strategy worked, but only to a limited extent. For nearly two thousand years, the people of Israel were scattered around the world, persecuted, forced to abandon their faith, expelled from countries, harassed, and even murdered by the millions. The few who remained in what came to be known as Palestine to almost everyone, lived in poverty in a barren, decrepit land in which hardly a tree grew, hardly a flower bloomed, and disease was rampant.

We traversed some miles of desolate country whose soil is rich enough but is given wholly to weeds – a silent, mournful expanse ... A desolation is here that not even imagination can grace with the pomp of life and action. We reached Tabor safely ... We never saw a human being on the whole route. We pressed on toward the goal of our crusade, renowned Jerusalem. The further we went the hotter the sun got and the more rocky and bare, repulsive and dreary the landscape became ... There was hardly a tree or a shrub anywhere. Even the olive and the cactus, those fast friends of a worthless soil, had almost deserted the country. No landscape exists that is more tiresome to the eye than that which bounds the approaches to Jerusalem ... Jerusalem is mournful, dreary and lifeless. I would not desire to live here. It is a hopeless, dreary, heartbroken land ...[13]

(Mark Twain, on his visit to the Land of Israel)

Despite the lowly state of the Jewish people and the lowly state of their ancestral homeland, they continued to pray with faces pointed to the Land of Israel. Every day, devout Jews would cry out to their Creator at least three times a day for the return to the Land of Israel. Most people, even many Jews, didn't believe that

Jerusalem – Mournful, Dreary And Lifeless: *Mark Twain on a journey through the Land of Israel in 1867 shortly before the Jewish return to the land began.*

the return to the Land was even a remote possibility. After all, what nation has ever been exiled from its land, bounced from country to country, suffered unparalleled horrors, yet despite everything, returned to reestablish itself again as a sovereign nation in its ancient homeland? Yet, as absurd as it seemed, for believing Jews, it was a given, the essence of being a Jew was to pray for the eventual and expected return.

> *Blow the great shofar (ram's horn) for our liberation, and raise up a miracle to gather our exiles, and gather us together from the four corners of the earth; blessed are You, O Lord, who gathers the dispersed of His people Israel.*

(From the *Amidah* prayer, said three times daily)

Sure enough, in the late 19th century, the people of Israel started to come back to their tiny piece of land at the crossroads of three great continents. It started out as very small groups of tens that eventually became hundreds and then thousands. Life was very difficult for them. At first there was no economy, little farming, and lots of diseases, including malaria. The challenge of returning to the homeland was overwhelming for some, but there was no turning back. The process continued. The Jewish pioneers drained the swamps and worked long hours to create agriculture. New cities were built. Old cities and towns were rebuilt. An economy was developed where there was none. Trees started to grow, the desert started to bloom, and the land began to give of its fruit once again. And guess what else started to happen in the 1920s as this amazing process was well underway? Immigrants from the neighboring Arab-inhabited lands flocked to this new Jewish country in the making, looking for opportunities in a growing economy. Joining together with some of their Arab brethren who already lived there, they began to agitate against their Jewish neighbors, sounding the Arab war cry of "Itbach al-Yahud!" (Kill the Jews). Terrible pogroms, or violent riots, were carried out by Arab mobs in the cities of Jerusalem, Tsfat (Safed), and Hebron. The scourge of rapes of Jewish women and the increasing fear of Arab snipers on the roads was ever-present and were interspersed with wild rampages of outright murder.

Our review of these early conflicts in the land that was then known to the world as Palestine brings us back to our previous discussion about the so-called Palestinians. The Arab residents in the Land of Israel in the early part of this century didn't refer to themselves as Palestinians. In fact, if you called yourself a Palestinian, you were most likely one of the Jewish residents. Most of the Arabs seemed to follow the lead of their religious and political leader, the Grand Mufti of Jerusalem, Haj (Muhammad Effendi) Amin al-Husseini, the radical pro-Nazi Muslim leader, scion of the influential Husseini family of Jerusalem. Husseini was an ardent Arab nationalist. The thought of creating a separate Arab nation called Palestine was the farthest thing from his

Holocaust Planning Session: *Haj Amin al-Husseini meets with Nazi kingpin Adolf Hitler.*

mind. No, he wanted to unite all of the Arabs as one nation and established the Arab Higher Committee, to work towards his stated goal of driving the "Zionists" out of the Land. Toward this end, he met with Adolf Hitler's second in command, Adolf Eichmann, in late 1937, when Eichmann visited Palestine to discuss the possibility of establishing concentration camps and deporting Jews to there. Husseini later met with Hitler, as well. His collaboration with the Nazis is well-documented.[14]

> *The Germans know how to get rid of the Jews. They have definitely solved the Jewish problem.*[15]
>
> (Haj Amin al-Husseini
> in Berlin, Germany, November 2, 1943)

Husseini's grand plans of developing his own final solution didn't come to fruition. Even though six million Jews were slaughtered by the Nazis, Husseini's great hopes of driving out their brethren from the Middle East never materialized as Israel's return soon turned into a return to Jewish sovereignty.

UN Partition Plan Of 1947

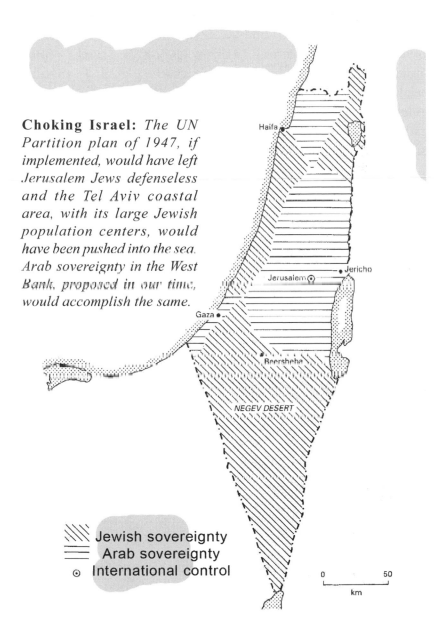

Choking Israel: *The UN Partition plan of 1947, if implemented, would have left Jerusalem Jews defenseless and the Tel Aviv coastal area, with its large Jewish population centers, would have been pushed into the sea. Arab sovereignty in the West Bank, proposed in our time, would accomplish the same.*

Haifa

Jerusalem

Jericho

Gaza

Beersheba

NEGEV DESERT

Jewish sovereignty
Arab sovereignty
International control

0   50
km

With the end of the League of Nations in 1945 after World War II, the British, who had been authorized to rule over Palestine since 1917, surrendered their mandate. The United Nations was established and the new body eventually gave its approval in 1948 for a truncated Jewish State of Israel, with its historic capital, Jerusalem, to be internationalized. Though its borders reflected only a small fraction of the historic Jewish homeland, it was a cause for celebration, as the sovereign nation of Israel officially returned to its Land after 1900 years of dispersion and national homelessness.

The Arabs rejected the vote and declared war on the nascent state. The new sovereign State of Israel declared its independence on May 15, 1948 and the Arabs, surrounding Israel on all sides, and heavily outnumbering its meager army, both in weaponry and soldiers, launched a coordinated war against Israel. The war was extremely painful, both in terms of deaths and territory lost to Israel's people. A full one percent of the population of the reestablished state fell in the fighting, half of

The Battle For Jerusalem 1948: *Jewish residents of Jerusalem's Old City surrender to Jordanian soldiers in 1948.*

whom were civilians. The historic, biblical, mountainous regions of Samaria and Judea and eastern Jerusalem had fallen into the hands of the newly independent Kingdom of Jordan, which had been established just twenty years earlier on the eastern side of the Jordan River. The southern region of Gaza was taken by the Egyptians and the Golan Heights on the country's northern peaks by the newly independent Republic of Syria.[16]

At the end of the war, Israel was left with a truncated state with a dangerous east to west bottleneck just nine miles wide. This fragile, almost indefensible situation continued for nineteen years, with the threats from the east, both stated and implicit growing greater every day.

We intend to open a general assault against Israel. This will be total war. Our basic aim will be to destroy Israel.[17]

(Egyptian President Gamal Abdel Nasser, May 26, 1967)

The sole method we shall apply against Israel is total war, which will result in the extermination of Zionist existence.[18]

(Egyptian Radio, Voice of the Arabs, May 18, 1967)

I, as a military man, believe that the time has come to enter into a battle of annihilation.[19]

(Syrian Defense Minister Hafez al-Assad, May 20, 1967)

The existence of Israel is an error which must be rectified ... Our goal is clear – to wipe Israel off the map.[20]

(Iraqi President Abdur Rahman Aref, May 31, 1967)

The result of these verbal attacks and the military maneuvers that accompanied them was the Six Day War in June of 1967. Once again attacked from all sides, Israel fought another valiant war of survival and the results were nothing short of miraculous. Israel recaptured the mountainous regions Judea and Samaria

Returning To The Wall – June 1967: *Israeli soldiers rejoice after the recapture of the Temple Mount's Western Wall in Jerusalem.*

(known to most of the world as the West Bank), with the historic, biblical cities of Bethlehem, Shiloh, Jericho, Shechem, Bethel, and Hebron. These places were the cradle of Western civilization, the sites where most of the biblical stories took place. Another result of the war was the recapturing of eastern Jerusalem, including the Temple Mount (Mount Moriah) and its famous Western Wall, which had often been called the Wailing Wall, because of the tears that had been shed there through the years of dispersion by Jews who somehow managed to come to pray at the site. Their tears were joined in spirit with the tears that were shed by those Jews who couldn't get there physically but cried daily over Zion's destruction. As an outcome of the fighting, Israel also recaptured the strategic Golan Heights in the north, the vast Sinai desert in the south, and the Gaza Strip region on the southwest coast.

The dangerous, fragile borders of Israel that had existed from 1948-1967 have been known to many as "The Auschwitz Borders", thus aptly titled as such by Israel's Foreign Minister

Abba Eban, in bitter memory of the notorious Nazi death camp of the same name:

> *We have openly said that the map will never again be the same as on June 4, 1967. For us, this is a matter of security and of principles. The June map is for us equivalent to insecurity and danger. I do not exaggerate when I say that it has for us something of a memory of Auschwitz. We shudder when we think of what would have awaited us in the circumstances of June 1967, if we had been defeated; with Syrians on the mountain and we in the valley, with the Jordanian army in sight of the sea, with the Egyptians who hold our throat in their hands in Gaza. This is a situation which will never be repeated in history.[21]*

(Abba Eban, Israeli Foreign Minister, UN Ambassador)

The Six Day War was a great victory for Israel, but not just because of the geographic strategic depth that it provided. The miraculous nature of the triumph affirmed the uniqueness of Israel, for what other nation but the original biblical nation wins a war in six days and on the Sabbath day they rest?

Furthermore, it was a rare, yet classic return to roots story, as the territories that Israel recovered from Jordanian occupation were the biblical heartland, Israel's raison d'être, its most powerful claim to the Land of Israel. It's important to remember that King David's unified kingdom was based in eastern Jerusalem, not in the relatively new coastal city of Tel Aviv. Samuel the Prophet grew up into prophecy in Shiloh in the heart of Samaria, not in the relatively new resort city of Netanya, while the Patriarchs and Matriarchs of Israel are buried in Hebron in Judea, not in the relatively new city of Petach Tikva. The region that the world likes to call the West Bank is in reality the biblical heartland of Israel and the cradle of Western, or Judeo-Christian civilization. Any Jew and any Christian who pressures Israel to surrender those areas is denying his or her roots and the biblically-based roots of Western Civilization.

If we are speaking about deep roots in the land, shouldn't we also address the origins and deep ties to the land of the Palestinians? After all, even if the Romans invented the name, aren't today's Palestinians a legitimate people with rights in their ancient homeland?

CHAPTER TWO

The New Palestinians

We must not forget that Messiah (Jesus) is a Palestinian,
the son of Mary the Palestinian.[1]
(Official PA newspaper Al-Hayat Al-Jadida
November 18, 2005)

Author: The Shaheed (martyr) President Yasser Arafat
used to say: Jesus was the first Palestinian Shaheed. I
heard him say that sentence many times.
PA TV Host: He (Jesus) was a Palestinian; no one
denies that.
Author: He (Jesus) was the first Palestinian Shaheed.
He (Arafat) attributed this Martyrdom to Palestine, as
well.[2]
From a program on PA TV: "This Is Our Religion"

The first Palestinian Shaheed? Was Jesus a Palestinian suicide bomber who blew up buses? Or was he perhaps one of those heroic Palestinian martyrs who ambush cars and shoot at babies from the side of the road? The fact that there were no buses or cars in those days is unimportant. Clearly, the fact that there were no Palestinians then is irrelevant, as well. When it comes to lies, deceitfulness, and the distortion of history, almost anything is acceptable for these new-age Palestinians – even ignoring the fact that the Romans created the word "Palestina", hoping to erase the names Israel and Judea off the map, exactly 136 years **after** Jesus was born.[3]

The Maestro Of Modern Terrorism: *PLO Chairman and PA President Yasser Arafat. Did he also create the Palestinian people?*

Some time ago, I participated in a news panel via Skype on CBN News, and in the last part of the show, the correspondent, Chris Mitchell, showed a feature segment in which he had asked random passersby in New York City's Times Square a very simple question – Where is Palestine? Despite the frequency with which that word appears in the news, hardly any of the interviewees could accurately answer the question.[4] It's probably safe to assume that if the question had been: "Who are the Palestinians?" the respondents would have been equally befuddled. This speaks volumes about the game of semantics that certain interested parties are playing in the media to deceive a public in the English-speaking world that doesn't really know the facts about Israel and the Middle East. From those efforts, we get terms like Palestinians and West Bank, terms that are merely politically-derived substitutes for the actual historical terms.

It's important to remember that these substitute terms didn't exist until the name-changes were made for nefarious purposes to deceive an unaware public. Many people who follow the news and are even supporters of Israel are unaware that "West

Bank" is a term that was only coined by the Arab nations after the Jordanian conquest of this area during Israel's War of Independence in 1948. The Jordanians (at that time still called Trans-Jordan, meaning "the other side of the Jordan River") gave it this name to distinguish it from the rest of the Jordanian kingdom, which was the East Bank of the Jordan River. Until then, the term West Bank had been unheard of, but the Arab nations, seeing the potential propaganda benefits, seized on the term as soon as the area was recaptured by Israel in 1967. The original and historically accurate names for these areas, used for several thousand years, are Samaria (Shomron in Hebrew), which is north of Jerusalem, and Judea (Yehuda), which is south of Jerusalem. This is the strategic, central hill country of Israel, where most of the biblical sites are located.[5]

The first rabbi to hold the title of Chief Rabbi of the Land of Israel, Rabbi Abraham Isaac Kook, of blessed memory, wrote extensively, not just about the return of Israel to its land, but also about the topic of personal self-improvement. Rabbi Kook emphasized that the first step in self-improvement is awareness that there is what to improve.[6] Often we don't like to admit that we are ignorant on a given topic, but that very awareness of our need to improve our behavior towards others is a vital first step towards self-improvement. This can be applied as well towards an improved understanding of public, national, and international issues, as well. The Palestinian issue is a prime example of public ignorance that needs to be corrected. It's critical to first recognize the shortcomings in our knowledge of the facts, then to get to work to fill in the gaps. I remember my first day in a college political science course. The young lecturer said to the class of about twenty students, "I am not inherently smarter than you. The only reason why I'm standing here and you're sitting opposite me is because I've done a lot more reading and spent many more nights in the library than you have." It was perhaps an oversimplification, but the message was clear as day and I have never forgotten it. By properly educating ourselves, we can acquire the ability to educate others, and when it comes to the contentious Middle East, learning the historical facts is a good start.

Just three years before the Six Day War, in May of 1964, the Arab League, which was comprised of fourteen Arab countries, had established the Palestine Liberation Organization (PLO), as a political/military body to deal directly with the problem of the Palestinian Arabs. The PLO's first leader was an Egyptian, Ahmed Shukairy. In 1969, the most notable leader of the PLO – Fatah leader Yasser Arafat – was elected chairman of the new organization with its immediate goal being to create a Palestinian people and use it as a tool to wipe "the Zionist entity" off the map. Up until that point, the term Palestinian had referred more to Jews than to Arabs or Muslims. My father-in-law was born in Jerusalem in 1939 to parents with deep multi-generational roots in the Land of Israel, nine years before the State of Israel was established. To this day, he continues to assert that, if there is such a thing, he is far more of a Palestinian than Cairo-born Arafat ever was. He repeatedly emphasizes that the only people who even used the term Palestinians to describe themselves were Jews and that most Arabs of the Land of Israel, who considered themselves part of "the Arab nation", refused to use the term Palestinians, until many years later, when it became politically expedient to do so.

Ten years after the PLO was founded, at the 1974 Rabat Summit of Arab nations, which included the PLO, it was decided to reaffirm the armed struggle against Israel, and a unanimous resolution was passed which, for the first time, declared the PLO to be the "sole legitimate representative of the Palestinian people." It also declared that the Arab world would accept any parts of the Land of Israel that Israel would decide to surrender peacefully. Thus, began the policy of shooting at Israel and bombing Israel with one hand, while simultaneously having "peace" negotiations with the other.[7]

We plan to eliminate the state of Israel and establish a

purely Palestinian state. We will make life unbearable for Jews by psychological warfare and population explosion ... We Palestinians will take over everything, including all of Jerusalem.[8]

(Yasser Arafat, PLO Chairman
Stockholm, 1996)

Peace by persuasion has a pleasant sound, but I think we should not be able to work it. We should have to tame the human race first, and history seems to show that that cannot be done.[9]

(Mark Twain)

It's always necessary to know the history in order to understand the present beyond the surreal world of media spin. The Palestinians that everyone speaks of are hardly an indigenous people deprived of their rights. However, the politicians of the world seem to accept otherwise. The Palestinian narrative has been adopted and promoted wholeheartedly by the purveyors of political correctness, those self-righteous denizens of the far-Left, for whom Israel had long ago ceased to be a fashionable cause. In fact, it is nearly impossible for a public figure to burst the indigenous, long-suffering Palestinian people bubble without being fiercely attacked by dogmatic leftists whose arrogance towards those who refute their arguments is only matched by their ignorance of the Middle Eastern facts on the ground.

Nonetheless, there are some notable exceptions, who have dared to defy the wrath of the pontifical Left on this issue. The Palestinian question received a surprising flurry of attention in the heat of the 2012 Presidential campaign season in the United States, when Republican candidates Newt Gingrich, Rick Santorum, and Herman Cain all pointed out the inconsistencies in the Palestinian narrative.

Remember there was no Palestine as a state. It was part of the Ottoman Empire. And I think that we've had an invented Palestinian people, who are in fact Arabs, and

39

An Invented People: *Presidential candidate and former House Speaker Newt Gingrich stated some historical truths that many people either don't know or prefer to ignore.*

---

were historically part of the Arab community, Gingrich said. And they had a chance to go many places. And for a variety of political reasons we have sustained this war against Israel now since the 1940s, and I think it's tragic.[10]

(Republican Candidate Newt Gingrich)

Those territories were conquered (by Israel) because of an aggressive attack on the part of Jordan and other countries. There are no Palestinians. This is Israeli land.[11]

(Republican Candidate Rick Santorum).

I think that the so-called Palestinian people have this urge for unilateral recognition because they see this president as weak.[12]

(Republican Candidate Herman Cain)

Perhaps some hard questions need to be asked of the promoters of the national rights of a State of Palestine:

- When in history did the ancient State of Palestine exist?
- What was the national language?
- What was its national currency?
- In what year did this state achieve its sovereignty and in which year did it lose its sovereignty?
- Who was the first president or monarch of this ancient country and in what year did he take office?

No "Palestinian" leader today can answer these questions because there are no answers, and the reason? There never was a sovereign country called Palestine!

The illusion of an indigenous, formerly sovereign Palestinian people is perhaps the greatest hoax of modern times and anyone who truly seeks peace and harmony between peoples anyplace on this planet, needs to recognize this fact of history, rather than play a cynical game of doublespeak, designed to deceive an uninformed public. Peace can only be achieved if we have a realistic understanding of who we are dealing with and what the competing ideologies are. There needs to be a clear definition of terms, starting with the term "peace."

Peace for us means the destruction of Israel. We are preparing for an all-out war, a war which will last for generations.[13]

(PLO Chairman Yasser Arafat,
Jordanian Television, September 13, 1993)

Incredibly, those words were spoken on September 13, 1993, the very same day that the PLO and Israel signed the Oslo Accords in a lively celebration of the vaunted peace process on the White House lawn. And what a day it was! In an event that was designed to get the maximal media exposure, PLO negotiator Mahmoud Abbas and Israeli Foreign Minister

Let's Make Peace: *President Bill Clinton oversees the handshake on the White House lawn between Prime Minister Yitzchak Rabin and PLO Chairman Yasser Arafat at the Oslo Accords ceremony. Was peace on the horizon?*

Shimon Peres signed the document for their respective sides at a ceremony on the White House lawn, witnessed by President Bill Clinton, Secretary of State Warren Christopher, Russian Foreign Minister Andrei Kozyrev, Israel's Prime Minister Yitzhak Rabin and PLO Chairman Yasser Arafat.

Negotiated in secret between Israel and the PLO, the Oslo Accords envisaged a withdrawal of Israeli forces from parts of the Gaza Strip, as well as Judea and Samaria (the West Bank), and their replacement by a Palestinian National Authority (PA). The PA would be given limited rule, to be known as autonomy, over the major Palestinian population centers in the West Bank and Gaza for a five-year interim period, during which further transfers of land to the PA would be discussed. The idea of a phased transition to Palestinian rule was intended to build mutual trust for negotiating a final-status agreement – the most difficult issues, namely Jerusalem, refugees, Israeli settlements, security, water rights and borders were purposefully left to the end in the hope that a successful interim period would make people on both sides more amenable to compromise.[14]

The first phase, which mainly consisted of Israeli withdrawal and transfer of land, cities, and towns in Judea, Samaria, and Gaza to the PA, was implemented, but it was a source of great political turmoil in an Israel that was fearful of what the second phase would bring in its wake. Sure enough, the Oslo Two agreement of September 1995 advanced agreements on security issues, PA elections, further transfer of land, transfer of civil power from Israel to the PA, trade conditions and release of Palestinian prisoners who had been jailed for past terrorist attacks on Israeli civilians. Israeli politicians like Shimon Peres and Yossi Beilin, the architects of the Oslo Accords, loudly proclaimed a "New Middle East", asserting that Israel needed to recognize that "times-they-were-a-changing", with the title of the old Bob Dylan song suddenly seeming appropriate to a Middle Eastern context. However, Israel was deeply divided and apprehensive about the new situation, especially since there were so many doubts about the sincerity of their new-found peace partners.

> *The Jihad (Islamic holy war against "non-believers")*
> *will continue, and Jerusalem is not (only) for the*
> *Palestinian people, it is for all the Muslim nation ..., you*
> *have to come and to fight and to start the Jihad to liberate*
> *Jerusalem.[15]*
>
> (PLO Chairman Yasser Arafat, May 10, 1994,
> speaking in a mosque in Johannesburg, South Africa)

Shortly afterwards, when word had gotten out about his peace-shattering speech, Arafat was approached by throngs of Western reporters who confronted him about the obvious contradiction of being committed to resolving differences of opinion peacefully and publicly calling for Jihad, or holy war to conquer Jerusalem for all of "the Muslim nation." He wrinkled his face with that sly smile that he was known for, and proclaimed, "I will continue my Jihad for peace!" It was an obvious oxymoron that none of the assembled journalists seemed to know how to respond to, but who could blame them?

An individual of no less stature than Israel's Foreign Minister Shimon Peres quickly jumped in a few days later to meet with Arafat and lovingly accept his explanation of the unfortunate "misunderstanding" in Johannesburg.[16]

The media concerns seemed to have been momentarily silenced by Arafat's quick-footed, though odd response as well as Peres's rush to kiss (or at least to shake hands) and make up, even though it was, in reality, a race to rescue his own peace-making reputation. Nonetheless, a large part of the Israeli public remained unconvinced about the arch-Jihadist's slip of the tongue. After all, this was still the same terrorist leader who had masterminded some of the worst terrorist massacres in Israel's history. Had he really abandoned terrorism since the signing of the Oslo Accords?

The Israeli concerns were heightened, when on the eve of the 1996 elections, Palestinian terrorist groups launched a string of horrific terrorist attacks, including bus bombings in Israel's major cities, killing and wounding scores of civilians. In one of those attacks alone, near the Jerusalem Central Bus Station, twenty-six people were murdered in a bus bombing orchestrated by the Hamas terrorist organization.[17]

It is widely believed that these attacks influenced the election results, as Shimon Peres was narrowly defeated by Benjamin Netanyahu. The illusion of Peres's new Middle East of peace and economic progress was exposed as the same old Middle East, but in a new and more dangerous form.

> *The Arabs are the same Arabs and the sea is the same sea.[18]*
>
> (Prime Minister Yitzchak Shamir, as quoted by Benjamin Netanyahu)

This of course referred to the historical Arab Muslim dream of driving the Jews into the sea. While the exact wording of the Shamir quote has been disputed by some, the message was clear.

The Fruit Of Oslo: *Bus bombings and roadside shootings killed and wounded many hundreds of Israeli civilians as the politicians negotiated the new era of peace.*

Despite what some self-proclaimed peace pundits have told us, the reality of the Arab world wanting to destroy Israel did not change after the Oslo Accords, but the strategy of achieving goals through negotiation as well as terrorism did. The central question for Israel in this new era seemed to be. How do you fight against terrorists who deny responsibility for terror attacks and claim to be peacemakers? A pattern had begun of terror attacks in which the heads of the Palestinian Authority would disavow involvement and the

He Was Soft-Spoken And Friendly, But He Knew How To Say No: *Prime Minister Yitzchak Shamir, who served from 1983-1984 and 1988-1992, was willing to talk and extend his hand in peace, but he made it clear that his principles weren't negotiable.*

leaders of Israel would demand that Arafat condemn the attack. Sometimes he would and sometimes he refused. Sometimes the attack would be carried out by Fatah or the al-Aqsa Martyrs' Brigades (now only under Arafat's unofficial leadership because he couldn't be officially seen to be advocating terrorism) and other times it would be Hamas or Islamic Jihad, but it didn't really matter which terrorist organization did it. The pattern was the same and the attacks continued.

Even so, a great portion of Israeli society from the political leadership to the cultural elites refused to consider that perhaps the golden calf of Israeli withdrawal was not the answer to the conflict. Just as the impulsive Israelites didn't stop to think logically about why they were dancing around a golden calf in the desert, the immature leftists of Peace Now continued their illogical race to give away Israel's biblical heartland, including Jerusalem.

> *For they have healed the hurt of the daughter of my people slightly, saying, Peace, peace – when there is no peace.*
>
> (Jeremiah 8:11)

Their argument goes something like this: If we give the Palestinians what they are demanding at the moment – an independent State of Palestine in Judea, Samaria, Gaza, and East Jerusalem as the capital city – they will be happy and will make no more demands on us. We will express our desire to live happily within the borders of pre-1967 Israel and once they see how magnanimous we are, wanting to give them an independent state, they will want to live peacefully alongside us. Or, as explained by one of secular Israel's cultural icons:

> *No idea has ever been defeated by force ... To defeat an idea, you have to offer a better idea, a more attractive and acceptable one. Thus, the only way for Israel to edge out Hamas would be to quickly reach an agreement with the Palestinians on the establishment of an independent*

state in the West Bank and Gaza Strip as defined by the 1967 borders, with its capital in East Jerusalem.[19]
(Israeli author Amos Oz, June 2010)

No idea has ever been defeated by force? Has this highly-educated Israeli ever heard of Nazism? Has he never heard of World War Two? Were the Nazis defeated by the appeasement of British Prime Minister Neville Chamberlain? Were the Nazis defeated when Chamberlain succumbed to Hitler's territorial desires and handed over to them the Sudetenland of Czechoslovakia?[20] The problem with this "path to peace" is that appeasement doesn't work. It didn't work in combating Nazi aggression in Europe and it doesn't work in the Middle East. Aside from the usurping of Israel's historical rights in its biblical heartland and placing Israel behind indefensible borders, the so-

Appeasement Doesn't Bring Peace: *British Prime Minister Neville Chamberlain returned from talks with Hitler and Mussolini and proclaimed the attainment of "Peace in our time".*

called Palestinians have made it quite clear in their Arabic speeches, and occasionally in English, but hardly ever in Hebrew, that they are not prepared to be satisfied with anything less than full Arab sovereignty in Jaffa, Safed, Haifa, and Lod. For those who aren't familiar with the map of Israel, those cities are all within pre-1967 Israel. Just as the Sudetenland wasn't Hitler's end goal, the principle has always been the same in our neck of the woods. The West Bank and Gaza was always the equivalent of the Sudetenland in Arafat's grand plan.

Both phases of the Oslo Accords transformed Israeli

attitudes towards the so-called Palestinians. Israeli media and schools made a serious and conscious effort to educate towards peace. Many objective observers have noted that Israeli educators and the media, as well as the Israel Defense Forces educational apparatus bent over backwards, even distorted the facts to show balance and understanding for the Palestinian narrative.

The Oslo II Agreement stated that:

> *Israel and the (Palestinian) Council will ensure that their respective educational systems contribute to the peace between the Israeli and Palestinian peoples and to peace in the entire region, and will refrain from the introduction of any motifs that could adversely affect the process of reconciliation.*[21]

However, the official Palestinian Authority-controlled television, which is basically an extension of the PA educational system, has continued to educate PA children that all of Israel is "Palestine," according to program translations provided by the Palestinian Media Watch.

A repeated message on the children's show "The Best Home," broadcast three times a week during the month of Ramadan, was that all Israeli cities are "occupied" Palestinian cities.

The PA TV host refers to cities in Israel alternately as "1948 occupied cities", "occupied cities", or "occupied territories." The Israeli cities described as Palestinian cities include Haifa, Jaffa, Acre – all of which are located on the coast of the Mediterranean Sea, and Lod and Ramle, located adjacent to Israel's Ben Gurion International Airport – not one of them in the West Bank.

On one program, a PA TV host tells a girl, "You live in Jerusalem. Do you visit the 1948 occupied (Israeli) cities?"

After she replies, "I've been to Hebron," the host continues, "No, Hebron is a city (in the Palestinian Authority) that we all can enter. The occupied cities – such as Lod, Ramle, Haifa, Jaffa, and Acre – have you visited them?"

The girl says, "I've been to Haifa and Jaffa," and the host

then tells viewers, "We hope all children of Palestine will be able to go to the occupied territories (within pre-1967 Israel), which we don't know and have never been able to see."[22]

In another report about the PA's official television programming for children, Walt Disney's daughter described Hamas as "pure evil" for creating a television show in which

Killing Zionists For Allah: *Palestinian television exploits Mickey Mouse to teach children the glory of Islamic terrorism.*

a Mickey Mouse-style character encourages terrorism against Israel and the US.

The al-Aqsa television station of Hamas, which dominates the Palestinian government, started showing "Tomorrow's Pioneers" last month. It is hosted by a presenter called Farfur, who dresses in a Mickey Mouse suit.

He advises children to drink their milk as well as encouraging what Israeli critics have described as "hate-filled propaganda" against the "Zionist occupation" of Palestine.

In one clip which has appeared on YouTube, a young viewer

speaking to Farfur by telephone recites a poem which includes the lines: "Rafah sings 'Oh, oh'. Its answer is an AK-47".

As the poem is being read out, Farfur pretends to shoot an assault rifle. Another child tells Farfur: "It is the time of death, we will fight a war."

Diane Disney Miller, 79, attacked the appropriation of Mickey Mouse, the comic character created in 1928 that became the Walt Disney Company's most familiar icon.

Ms. Miller, the only surviving child of Walt Disney who died in 1966, told the New York Daily News:

> *Of course I feel personal about Mickey Mouse, but it could be Barney as well.*
>
> *It's not just Mickey. It's indoctrinating children like this, teaching them to be evil. The world loves children and this is just going against the grain of humanity ... What we're dealing with here is pure evil and you can't ignore that.*

In the show, Farfur's co-host is a young girl called Saraa who speaks about the struggle against Israel and the US. Farfur tells children they must pray in the mosque five times a day until there is "world leadership under Islamic leadership."[23]

Throughout Benjamin Netanyahu's administration in the late 1990s, this non-peaceful behavior, otherwise known as incitement to terrorism, on the part of the Palestinian peace partners, continued and Netanyahu established the condition of "reciprocity", which hadn't existed up to that point. His predecessors Yitzchak Rabin and Shimon Peres simply hadn't insisted on the other side meeting its obligations as written in the Oslo Accords. For them, the goal had overruled the means. It didn't matter that the PA was launching or encouraging or at the very least allowing terrorist attacks against Israeli civilians emanating from its autonomous areas, as long as the sacred peace march of Israeli withdrawals moved forward.

> *You cannot make peace with open eyes.*[24]
>
> (Israeli President Shimon Peres, June 2012)

Certainly, if we had our eyes open on the road to peace at Oslo, we wouldn't have had the trauma of the terrorism and wars that we've experienced in recent years. The hundreds of Israeli civilian victims of terrorist attacks in the early to mid-1990s were often insensitively referred to as "sacrifices of peace" by Yitzchak Rabin, Shimon Peres, and other political leaders, a cynical term implying that this was a necessary product of the peace-making process and that it was unreasonable to complain too much about the attacks or to demand too strenuously that the PA end the attacks. To his credit, Bibi (his nickname) Netanyahu began to change both the avalanche of unlimited concessions and the ongoing insensitivity to the terror victims. However, he didn't end the withdrawal process, saying that he was bound by the Oslo Accords that were signed by his predecessors and that he would try to limit the damage. By saying that, Netanyahu was in effect tying his hands and undercutting his stated demand for reciprocity.

Despite this change in approach from the previous administration, Bibi's tough words weren't enough. In October of 1998, he accepted President Bill Clinton's invitation to attend a summit with the PA and American leadership at the secluded Wye River Conference Center in Wye River, Maryland. On October 23, 1998, the Wye Memorandum was signed by Netanyahu and Arafat, with Clinton as the key witness. As stipulated in the agreements, Israel withdrew from all territory it was required to transfer to the Palestinian Authority within the timetable. However, Israel did not see reciprocal steps being taken by the PA. Therefore, Israel believed that the Palestinian Authority's promises to implement its share of responsibilities under the Wye River Memorandum were not serious, and the agreement's understandings and goals were not implemented, with the exception of the Israeli withdrawals, which were carried out more or less on schedule.[25]

In 1999, Netanyahu's governing coalition collapsed, leading to new elections, which were won by the left-wing Labor Party headed by Ehud Barak. During the election campaign, Barak had promised to end Israel's controversial 22-year-long stay in Southern Lebanon within a year. On May 24, 2000, he followed through on that pledge.[26]

In the dark of night and under Hezbollah fire, Israel withdrew from Southern Lebanon, abandoning its Lebanese Christian militia allies and leaving them dependent on the mercy of the Hezbollah terrorists. This was only one controversial aspect of the withdrawal, as Barak was essentially abandoning southern Lebanon to the Hezbollah, which subsequently established its terrorist base and total domination in the southern part of the country, from where, as of 2012, an estimated 100,000-200,000 missiles were pointed at Israel's major cities.[27] The Hebrew play-on-words "Ehud Barach", literally meaning, "Ehud ran away" haunts him to this day, as the Hezbollah terrorists viewed the Israeli escape under fire as a great victory for their dominance in Lebanon. Meanwhile, the Hezbollah threat from the north grows ever greater.

With full autonomy in seven Arab-populated cities of Judea and Samaria and cities in Gaza already handed over to the PA by his two predecessors, Prime Minister Barak set about the task of seeking a final status agreement between Israel and the PA. While Netanyahu had withdrawn from vast portions of Judea and Samaria, he had appeared to do so reluctantly, always claiming that he was handshackled by the Oslo Accords and duty-bound to carry out its obligations. Even at Wye, his lack of enthusiasm was evident and he appeared to be succumbing to intense pressure being placed on him by the American administration.

Unlike Netanyahu, Barak appeared to be pushing forward the diplomatic process from conviction that it was the right thing to do for the sake of Israel. The Barak government quickly resumed peace negotiations with the PLO, stating that "Every attempt (by the State of Israel) to keep hold of this area (the West Bank and Gaza) as one political entity, leads, necessarily, to either a nondemocratic or a non-Jewish state. Because if the

Palestinians vote, then it is a binational state, and if they don't vote it is an apartheid state."[28]

This debate over the fate of the areas recaptured by Israel in the Six Day War of 1967 rages within Israel to this day. While most Israelis agree that the status quo will not ultimately be the long-term resolution, a wide array of plans have been put forth to resolve the challenge of a large and hostile Arab population living in the heartland of Israel. Some say that Israel must retain these areas for a variety of reasons. Aside from Israel's historical bond or religious connection to these areas, proponents of this view usually cite the strategic threat of allowing a terrorist-dominated entity to dominate the mountainous regions of Samaria that overlook Tel Aviv and Ben Gurion International Airport. Meanwhile, those who want to part with these areas point to what they see as a serious demographic threat to Israel's continued viability as a Jewish state if Israel retains the post-1967 areas. They assert that a rapidly increasing Arab population in these areas, were they to be given the right to vote, would quickly put an end to Israel, voting the country out of existence.

Camp David Fun, But No Deal: *President Bill Clinton hosts Prime Minister Ehud Barak and PA President Yasser Arafat at the Camp David II Peace Summit.*

There are many others who vehemently disagree with this view, pointing out that the Jewish population in Judea and Samaria is the fastest growing population in the entire country and is, in fact, outpacing the Arab growth.

In any event, Barak accepted the former premise and upon entering office, began to push for final status talks, claiming that the time was right to resolve all of the outstanding issues with the Palestinian Authority and to arrive at a final settlement of all issues. President Bill Clinton decided to play ball, announcing his invitation to Barak and Arafat on July 5, 2000, to come to the Camp David retreat to continue their negotiations on the Middle East peace process. There was a hopeful precedent in the 1978 Camp David Accords where President Jimmy Carter had succeeded in brokering a peace agreement between Egypt,

The Unattainable Model: *US President Jimmy Carter, flanked by Israeli Prime Minister Menachem Begin and Egyptian President Anwar Sadat at the signing ceremony. The second Camp David summit was modeled after the first, but despite good intentions on the part of President Clinton and Prime Minister Barak, it was destined for failure from the start.*

represented by President Anwar Sadat, and Israel, represented by Prime Minister Menachem Begin.

As we have already discussed, the Oslo Accords of 1993, sealed between the later assassinated Israeli Prime Minister Yitzhak Rabin and PLO Chairman Yasser Arafat, had provided that agreement should be reached on all of the outstanding issues between the Palestinian and Israeli sides – the so-called final status settlement – within five years of the implementation of Palestinian autonomy. However, the interim process put in place under Oslo had fulfilled neither Israeli nor Palestinian expectations, and when news first came out about Clinton's plans for a high-profile end-the-conflict summit, Arafat argued against it, saying that the Camp David II summit was premature.[29] Did Arafat really believe that, or were there other serious, unstated issues preventing him from wholeheartedly going to Camp David? Was full and complete peace, from his perspective, an unattainable option? Despite that proverbial "elephant in the room", Prime Minister Ehud Barak, PA Chairman Yasser Arafat, and President Bill Clinton, with great public fanfare and with massive media attention, all traveled to the summit at Camp David with high hopes and many unanswered questions.

CHAPTER THREE

The Summer Summit
To End All Summits

Peace if possible, truth at all costs.[1]

(Martin Luther)

Peace has always been a valued goal, but can it be attained in every situation? Furthermore, can true peace be achieved based on a falsehood? The British Prime Minister Neville Chamberlain's declaration after his meeting with Adolf Hitler comes to mind – "Peace in our time" – shortly before the Nazi occupation of Czechoslovakia.[2] Despite the great fanfare, this announcement of peace was actually the precursor to World War Two, one of the bloodiest wars in history, but also one of the most justifiable. Could it have been avoided through a more realistic approach to the dangers and the evil that the free world was facing?

We should also remember US Secretary of State Henry Kissinger's famous "Peace is at hand" declaration, which preceded some of the worst violence in the Vietnam War.[3] In recent years, we have heard many similar quotes from Israeli peace advocate and statesman Shimon Peres. In the aftermath of Peres's many dramatic pronouncements heralding peace and the so-called "new Middle East", we have seen the worst waves of terrorism in Israel's history, coupled with an increasing frequency of wars. So the question remains with us and it needs to be asked – Does unrealistic talk of peace lead to the opposite?

While there have been many summits on the topic of Middle East peace, it certainly wouldn't be inaccurate to call the Camp David II Summit, or Camp David 2000, the summit to end all summits. After some seven years of autonomy in the Palestinian Authority, during which time Yasser Arafat and his cohorts turned the faucet of terrorism on and off as they wished and continued their incitement to hatred and murder in their educational system and media, Prime Minister Ehud Barak inexplicably announced that the timing was right for new comprehensive peace talks to achieve a final status deal. President Bill Clinton agreed and issued the invitation to what was hoped to be an historic summit to arrive at a permanent settlement of the conflict.

The setting, at the Presidential retreat in Camp David, Maryland, wasn't an accident, as the previous Camp David Summit in 1978 had been considered a roaring success story, with the signing of the Camp David Accords, leading Israel's Prime Minister Menachem Begin and Egypt's President Anwar Sadat to the historic signing of the first peace treaty between Israel and an Arab neighbor. The two main accomplishments reported at that summit were that Israel had agreed to a full withdrawal from the vast Sinai desert that it had captured from Egypt in the Six Day War of 1967 and that the two sides had agreed to finalize the peace treaty, which was officially signed in 1979. In addition, a Framework for Peace

All Smiles In The Search For Peace: *President Anwar Sadat and Prime Minister Menachem Begin greet each other at Camp David, as President Jimmy Carter looks on approvingly.*

in the Middle East was agreed to concerning the issue of the Palestinians. Sadat claimed that this statement of principles was needed to defend him against charges in the Arab world that he was striking a separate peace deal with the hated "Zionist entity."

Up until Sadat's November 7, 1977 lightning visit to meet Begin and address the Israeli Knesset (Parliament) in Jerusalem, the thought of an Arab leader making peace with Israel had been considered nothing short of treasonous. The Sadat visit came about after he had delivered a speech in Egypt stating that he would travel to anywhere, "even Jerusalem," to discuss peace. That speech led the Begin government to declare that, if Israel thought that Sadat would accept such an invitation, that Sadat would be welcome to visit Jerusalem and to address the Knesset.[4] After having lost the vast Sinai desert in the Six Day War of 1967 and failing to get it back in the Yom Kippur War of 1973, Sadat was said to have felt great humiliation and loss of honor in an Arabic culture in which honor is paramount. Seeking to restore Arab honor (and his own at the same time) by regaining Sinai, after having failed to do so militarily, Sadat took a calculated personal risk by visiting Jerusalem as an honored guest of the State of Israel.

However, Anwar Sadat was not the only Middle Easterner imperiling his political standing, as there were serious political risks for Prime Minister Begin, as well. Begin had been elected in 1977 after years in the political opposition and was known to strongly favor the settlement movement of Jews reclaiming and rebuilding Jewish communities in territories that had fallen into Israel's hands in the Six Day War of 1967, a defensive war in which Israel was attacked on all sides by its Arab neighbors. Surrendering the entire Sinai was an enormous concession for Israel, and especially for Begin, that was hardly appreciated or valued by any of the parties to the talks. After capturing Sinai in a defensive war, this was a region in which Israel had begun staking much of its future development, both economic and demographic. Settling northeastern Sinai was an idea that had been promoted by the previous Labor Party-led government at the urging of then Defense Minister Moshe Dayan.[5] The idea of developing Sinai was subsequently proposed in a document on Israeli policy in Judea and Samaria written by Labor Party MK Yisrael Galili, drafted to bridge the gap between hardliners and moderates in the Labor Party, who had differing views on developing the recently captured territories.[6]

The beautiful Sinai, with its rich coral reefs, blue sea, and biblical history, and at 23,000 square miles in area, nearly three times as large as the 1967 State of Israel, was seen as a potential magnet for tourists from Israel and from around the world. This dream never went far beyond the planning stages, but in the realm of energy, Israel quickly put its ingenuity to work, developing the Alma oil field and Sadot gas field, valued at more than $100 billion. Had the Jewish State kept the oil fields with the reserves it had discovered in 1973, it would have meant energy independence for Israel, as well as the possibility of becoming an oil-exporting country.[7]

Furthermore, Israel saw an opportunity to spread out its densely populated waistline by settling the desert and making it bloom. It built several embryonic communities in Sinai, including what soon became a thriving town in northeastern Sinai called Yamit. All of this occurred under the more left-wing Labor government that preceded the rise to power of Menachem Begin's more nationalistic Likud in 1977. As negotiations progressed leading up to and during the first Camp David Summit, Begin had to stand up to those supporters for whom settlement was an almost sacred value, deeply rooted in both Judaism and Zionism. Though Begin's emphasis and his heartfelt commitment was to the challenge of settling Judea, Samaria, and all of Jerusalem, he faced fierce criticism from nationalists for even talking about giving away national assets in Sinai and destroying growing Jewish communities, all for a written promise of peace.

Despite the personal and political risks, and after thirteen days of intensive and often tense negotiations, the leaders concluded the 1978 Camp David Summit with smiles and hugs, and they received the 1978 Nobel Peace Prize for their efforts. The Camp David Summit stood alone as the singular peace-making event for many years. Even though it remained a presidential retreat, when Camp David was mentioned in succeeding years, it brought to mind the peace agreement between the longtime adversaries in the Middle East. It remained this way until Clinton, Barak, and Arafat decided to take their own stab at reaching an elusive peace agreement that would end the Israel-Palestinian conflict once and for all. It was hoped by the participants that the Carter-Sadat-Begin precedent would still be a good omen for success twenty-two years later when Clinton, Barak, and Arafat returned, seeking to repeat historical precedent.

This time around, the concept was the same – a series of meetings between the two leaders and their staff – with American guidance, encouragement, and pressure – to reach a ground-breaking agreement. As in the first Camp David Summit, the idea was to take as much time as was needed to get to the intended results. However, and unlike the first Camp David Summit, these negotiations would be based on an all or nothing approach. In other words, "nothing was considered agreed and binding until everything was agreed." Small steps of progress were not the goal. The goal was to finally and permanently end the conflict by reaching an all-inclusive agreement that would encompass all major issues and would not avoid the tough ones like Jerusalem and the Temple Mount, security, territory, settlements, refugees, and the right of return, which referred to the perceived right of Palestinian Arab refugees and their descendants to immigrate to Israel.

According to most reports, Barak came to the negotiations sincerely looking to end the conflict and was prepared to go a long way toward meeting Arafat's demands. He is reported to have offered to surrender an eventual 94% of Judea and Samaria and 100% of Gaza for a Palestinian state, not including Jerusalem. This bold move would have demanded the destruction and expulsion of

Once Known As The Wailing Wall: *Jewish women praying in the year 1910 at the Western Wall of the Temple Mount in Jerusalem, where for centuries Jews have cried over the end of Israel's sovereignty in the capital city.*

63 Jewish communities. While it's doubtful that ideology guided Barak's desire to preserve the few settlement blocs that would have been included in the 6% of Judea and Samaria that would have been retained for Israel, there were serious security issues for the rest of the country that he believed would mandate Israel's continued control of these areas. However, it should be pointed out that the security problem of giving away the high peaks in Samaria went well beyond protecting the 6%. Surrender of 94% to the PA would have meant giving Hamas, Islamic Jihad and Fatah terrorists the ability to rain rockets down onto Ben Gurion International Airport at will, thereby shutting it down in a matter of days, hours, or even minutes. In addition to the lack of concern about the very real issue of abandoning the Jewish residents of these areas, there was a disturbing lack of security responsibility on the part of Barak, as evidenced by his willingness to rely on the terrorist organizations to guarantee Israel's security. Another

aspect of the Israeli plan would have required the building of a new major road linking the West Bank and Gaza Strip by an elevated highway and an elevated railroad running through the Negev, ensuring safe and free passage for Palestinians from one part of their state to the other. This highway would have been under the sovereignty of Israel, and Israel reserved the right to close the highway to passage in case of emergency.[8] The real purpose of course, was to create Palestinian territorial contiguity between Judea, Samaria, and Gaza.

When it came to territory, PA objections centered on the fact that Israel wasn't offering them a full, 100% of Judea and Samaria. As far as they were concerned, a precedent had been established at the first Camp David summit twenty-two years prior, when Israel had surrendered 100% of the vast Sinai desert to Egypt. The PA was demanding no less for their independent state. They also claimed to be very disturbed by the lack of actual territorial contiguity between the West Bank and Gaza. The Israel security access was decried because of the hardship that the Arabs claimed it would impose on families. This claim, in the midst of ongoing PA-sponsored terrorism and incitement, wasn't very credible and belied their real concern, the question that they were careful not to ask publicly – How dare Israel disrupt coordination and the flow of weapons between the Fatah, Hamas, and Islamic Jihad terrorists?

These words are written only half tongue-in-cheek, for the reality of terrorist coordination was and continues to be a real and present danger, as evidenced by the long list of terrorist attacks on Israeli civilians. Many people in the West – Americans, Europeans, and some Israelis as well – don't recognize the extent of the cooperation between the various Islamic terrorist organizations. Each group exploited the Oslo arrangements of Palestinian-controlled autonomous cities to build bomb factories and to smuggle in weapons. Yes, there are internal rivalries between the various terrorist organizations in the Land of Israel. Furthermore, the rivalries are intense between the main ethnic antagonists throughout the Middle East, especially between Sunni Muslims and Shiite Muslims, but these are not relevant to the Palestinians, who are almost entirely Sunni. Their internal rivalries are mostly power struggles, but they are all sworn enemies of Israel and the West and the competition between the various terrorist organizations centers around each group's desire to show the people that they are launching the greatest resistance to the "Zionist occupation". That desired perception in the public eye is what brings them more adherents and more soldiers on the ground, because violence against the Zionists is what the Palestinian man or woman in the street wants.

Rather than negotiating about the territorial differences at Camp David, the Palestinian Authority simply rejected the generous Israeli offer, even though it went way beyond what any Israeli leader had ever suggested in the past. Many Israelis and friends of Israel found it incredible that Prime Minister Barak was prepared to hand over such a large percentage of Israel's historic, biblical heartland for a very questionable peace commitment from the other side. Given the PA's strategy of combining terrorist warfare with simultaneous peace negotiations, they rightly questioned the sincerity of the PA and its residents.

Israel will not negotiate under fire and under terror. If we do that, we will never reach peace.[9]
(Prime Minister Ariel Sharon – Barak's successor,
June 26, 2001)

Despite the sharp disagreement over the issue of territory at Camp David, it wasn't what eventually brought the negotiations to an end. Nor was it the dispute over Israel's legitimate security concerns. For example, the Israeli negotiators, concerned about realistically protecting their fellow citizens in a country smaller than New Jersey, proposed that Israel be allowed to maintain radar stations inside the Palestinian state, and be allowed to use its airspace. Israel also wanted the right to deploy troops on Palestinian territory in the event of an emergency, and the stationing of an international force in the Jordan Valley. Palestinian authorities would maintain control of border crossings under temporary Israeli observation. Israel would maintain a permanent security presence along 15% of a Palestinian-Jordanian border. Israel also demanded that the Palestinian state be demilitarized with the exception of its paramilitary security forces for internal needs, that it would not make alliances (with enemies such as Iran) without Israeli approval or allow the introduction of foreign forces east of the Jordan River, and that it dismantle terrorist groups.[10]

This last demand was indeed absurd, as the PA had in effect been doing just the opposite, by turning the faucet of terrorism on and off as it saw fit, using it as a negotiating tactic, even launching its own attacks through its surrogate organizations, such as Fatah and the al-Aqsa Brigade, then disavowing all responsibility for such attacks. One of Israel's strongest security litmus tests was that once the agreement was reached, that Arafat would declare the conflict over, and make no further demands. After all, if the goal was truly to make peace, and not to destroy Israel in pieces, or stages, there would be no objection to such an Israeli demand. Israel also wanted water resources in the West Bank to be shared by both sides and remain, at least in the near future, under Israel's experienced management and expertise.

The Israeli negotiating team arrived at Camp David with a comprehensive plan, stating their demands, but being prepared to negotiate and compromise in good faith. On the other hand, it was apparent to everyone who was not a member of Arafat's team that for the PA, compromise was not on the agenda. In a rare candid moment, Mahmoud Abbas, one of the leading PA negotiators, said that even before the summit the Palestinians had "made clear to the Americans that the Palestinian side is unable to make concessions on anything." He also maintained that the whole process was some sort of a trap.[11]

While the Camp David process seemed to be going nowhere on the issues of territory and security, on the outside and in the media, the days were flying by and the impression of progress was being broadcast to the world. It made sense, for what else could the parties be doing all that time at the presidential retreat, if not making progress? The world listened for days to the reports coming out of Camp David, waiting with baited breath for each new press release and White House released photos showing the friendly camaraderie and good-spirited, yet intensely serious negotiations taking place. The entire press corps was waiting for the headline, for the conclusion, for the joint press conference heralding the new era in the Middle East that had finally arrived. Despite the up and down negotiations mixed with terrorist attacks and lack of trust, people were hopeful that with the perceived hard-line Netanyahu out of the picture, the promise of a peace could yet be fulfilled, and Camp David, it seemed, was the place to do it.

Sadly for many, the announcement never came, but a different, more stunning announcement did hit the airwaves. The Camp David Summit was over and had ended with no agreement. The negotiations had failed, but not due to the disputes over territory and security, rather the big issue that everyone had been avoiding since the Sadat-Begin Camp David summit in 1978 – Jerusalem. At that time, President Jimmy Carter had invited the two leaders, planning to stay for three days and possibly close to a week. Carter had no idea whether his summit would succeed, only that the stakes were high – four wars in three decades, with the likelihood of further violence – "We never dreamed we'd be there through thirteen intense and discouraging days," he wrote later, "with success in prospect only during the final hours."[12] Yes, it lasted for a full thirteen days, but according to most of the participants, it ended successfully. What was the reason why the first Camp David Summit ended in agreement and this one failed? Time Magazine State Department Correspondent Christopher Ogden shared some insights:

> *Unfortunately, Yasser Arafat is no Anwar Sadat, the late Egyptian President whose presence was felt – and missed – when the Camp David peace talks collapsed last week.*

And not just unfortunately for Israel and the United States. Arafat's Arab supporters wanted the Palestinian leader to make no concessions on Jerusalem and no significant territorial compromise, and he did not. Unlike Sadat, he thought small; instead of bridging the Arab-Israeli chasm, he sent negotiations back to the drawing board ...[13]

The Camp David 2000 summit foundered on the status of Jerusalem. The 1978 summit almost did as well, but in that case, the three sides eventually came up with language which kicked the issue all the way down the road to Camp David II. However, there was no postponing such decisions this time: Arafat had reiterated his intention to unilaterally declare a Palestinian state by September 13.

Clinton and Barak worked heroically, as had Carter and Begin. They were tireless, inventive and flexible, amazingly so in the case of Barak, whose political position in Israel was far less secure than Begin's was in 1978. The key difference lay in what Sadat and Arafat were willing to do. Sadat arrived at and left Camp David dangerously isolated from his Arab brethren. He had not consulted with them before going to Jerusalem or before signing the Camp David I pact, which Arabs considered a sellout. A hero to the West, he was shunned at home and three years later was assassinated by Arab nationalists. Arafat, on the other hand, was given a loud and heroic welcome when he returned with nothing. Nothing, that is, except a likely guarantee he'd avoid dying in a hail of bullets.[14]

Arafat's reluctance to come to Camp David didn't stem from the invitation being "premature" nor was it a question of timing. The negotiations broke up over the issue of Jerusalem, but, in truth the negotiations never had a chance, and that's why Jerusalem was the break-up issue. Arafat knew that it would be. Firstly, let's examine what happened according to this general description of what actually transpired, with several slight modifications made for the purpose of linguistic clarity or historical accuracy.

The Palestinians demanded complete sovereignty over East

Jerusalem and its holy sites, in particular, the Muslim sites al-Aqsa Mosque and the Dome of the Rock, which are located on the Temple Mount, and the dismantling of all Israeli neighborhoods in Jerusalem built over the Green Line (the imaginary dividing line separating the areas recaptured by Israel in the Six Day War of 1967). The Palestinian position, according to Mahmoud Abbas, at that time Arafat's chief negotiator:

> *All of East Jerusalem should be returned to Palestinian sovereignty. The Jewish Quarter and Western Wall should be placed under Israeli authority, not Israeli sovereignty, as an open city with cooperation on municipal services.*

Israel proposed that the Palestinians be granted "custodianship," though not sovereignty, on the Temple Mount, with Israel retaining control over the Western Wall, the western retaining wall of the ancient wall that surrounded the Temple Mount, and one of the most sacred sites in Judaism outside of the Temple Mount itself. Israeli negotiators also proposed the Palestinians be granted administration, but not sovereignty, over the Muslim and Christian Quarters of the Old City, with the Jewish and Armenian Quarters remaining in Israeli hands, and indicated readiness to consider total Palestinian sovereignty over the Muslim and Christian Quarters. According to this proposal, Palestinians would have been granted administrative control over all Islamic and Christian holy sites, and would be allowed to raise the Palestinian flag over them. A passage linking northern Jerusalem to Islamic and Christian holy sites would be annexed by the Palestinian state.

Concerning Jewish settlements in Judea and Samaria (the West Bank), the Israeli team proposed annexing to Israel settlements within the West Bank beyond the Green Line (the imaginary pre-1967 dividing line), such as Ma'ale Adumim, Givat Ze'ev, and Gush Etzion. Israel proposed that the Palestinians merge certain eastern Jerusalem Arab neighborhoods that had been annexed to Jerusalem just after 1967 (such as: Abu Dis, Elazariya, Anata, A-Ram, and eastern Sawahre) to create the city of Al-Quds (Jerusalem in Arabic), which would serve as the capital of Palestine. Israeli neighborhoods within East Jerusalem would remain under Israeli sovereignty. Outlying Arab neighborhoods of Jerusalem would come under Palestinian sovereignty, and core Arab neighborhoods would remain under Israeli sovereignty, but would gain autonomous powers. Palestinian Jerusalem would be run by a Palestinian civilian administration, with the possibility of merging it to Israeli Jerusalem, in which case Palestinian Jerusalem would be governed by a Palestinian branch municipality within the framework of an Israeli higher municipal council.[15]

If your head is spinning after hearing all of those detailed proposals, don't worry about your comprehension. Your head is okay, but the confusing jigsaw puzzle that was proposed by Barak's negotiating team as a peace plan was severely lacking, both in moral clarity and administrative clarity. However, that wasn't the reason why it was rejected by Palestinian negotiators.

Palestinians objected to the lack of sovereignty (they were only offered administrative control) over Islamic holy sites (meaning that those were legally still under Israeli sovereignty), while Israel would be able to retain sovereignty over Jewish holy sites. They also objected to Israel retaining sovereignty over certain culturally or religiously significant Arab neighborhoods in Jerusalem (such as Sheikh Jarrah, Silwan and At Tur), and to the right of Israel to keep Jewish neighborhoods that it built over the Green Line in East Jerusalem, which the Palestinians claimed block the contiguity of the Arab neighborhoods in East Jerusalem.[16]

To understand why the issue of Jerusalem was sure to cause a blow-up, we need to understand the fact that nobody wants to admit. The struggle over the Land of Israel, and in particular, Jerusalem, is a religious war that cannot and will not be resolved through compromise or negotiations. The details of negotiation discussed above pale in comparison to the real obstacles obstructing Middle East peace, obstacles that are not grasped by sincere, but misguided leaders. One well-intended, but hopelessly naive, American politician was once heard commenting, "If we could just get them to sit down together and discuss this like good Christians, we could help them to achieve peace." The problem was that he was ignoring several basic truisms that have long dogged peace-seekers in the Middle East:

- The Jews and almost all of the Arabs are not Christians.
- Many Christians believe in the same biblical principles that the Jews believe in, principles that are not accepted by most of the Muslim world.
- Sometimes deep, religious conflicts cannot be resolved through compromise.

Why is it that the Jewish world cannot accept and will not accept the surrender of Jewish sovereignty over Jerusalem, especially the Old City, where the Temple Mount and the Western Wall are located?

For the simple answer to that question, all that one has to do is to find the root of the principle of Jewish sovereignty in the Land of Israel in the all-time bestseller, The Bible:

The Lord said to Abram, Go from your land, from your relatives, and from your father's house to the land that I will show you. And I will make of you a great nation ...
(Genesis 12:1-2)

The Land of Israel was and is that land. The heart of the Land of Israel was and is Jerusalem, where Israel became a great nation. Jerusalem is mentioned 700 times in the Tanach, or the complete Jewish Bible, but it's not only the Jewish narrative. The great gentile King Cyrus of Persia, who speaks in the following verse, enabled the building of the second Holy Temple in Jerusalem, and understood that Jerusalem is the heart and soul of the nation of Israel, and the roots of that heritage have resonated for all of Western civilization.

*Whoever is among you of His entire people, may God be
with him, and let him go up to Jerusalem which is in Judah
and build the Temple of the Lord, God of Israel – He is the
God! – which is in Jerusalem.*

(Ezra 1:2-3)

After the 369 years that Shiloh had been Israel's capital
city over 3,000 years ago came to an end, King David went forth
to establish the unified Kingdom of Israel, with its capital in
Jerusalem. That is where the magnificent Holy Temple was built,
which was the center of Jewish worship until its destruction by
Nebuchadnezzar, after which it was rebuilt on the very same spot
where it had once stood. The platform on the small Jerusalem
mountain where it stood is called the Temple Mount. After the
Second Temple was destroyed by the Roman conquerors some
2000 years ago, most of the Jews were exiled from their land,
but whenever and wherever they have prayed, they have always
faced the Land of Israel. When in the Land of Israel, they have
always faced Jerusalem in prayer. When in Jerusalem, all eyes
point to the Temple Mount. When on the Temple Mount, they
face the Holy of Holies, which was the holiest spot in the Temple.
It's relevant to note that when Muslims pray, they face in the
direction of Mecca, which is located in Saudi Arabia, with their
rear ends facing the Holy of Holies, but we'll speak more about
the reasons for that later.

In short, and despite Ehud Barak's recklessly generous offer
in 2000, sovereignty over the city of Jerusalem and the Temple
Mount are not issues that Israel can ever compromise on, because
to give up Israeli sovereignty over Jerusalem would be to deny
who we are, our very essence.

*And spread over us a sukkah of Your peace. Blessed are
You O Lord, who spreads out a sukkah of peace over us,
over the entire people Israel, and over Jerusalem.*
(From the Sabbath evening prayers)

The sukkah is the flimsy hut that Jews erect adjacent to

Rear Ends To The Holy Of Holies: *Muslims pray on the Temple Mount in Jerusalem. When Jews pray anywhere in the world, they face the Land of Israel. When Jews pray in the Land, they face Jerusalem. When Jews pray in Jerusalem, they face the Temple Mount. When Jews pray on the Temple Mount, they face the Holy of Holies, the heart of the Temple. Muslims in prayer face Mecca in Saudi Arabia, where Muhammad lived.*

their homes for the seven-day holiday of Sukkot (the Feast of Tabernacles). We eat in it and many sleep in it in remembrance of the

The Temple Mount And The Western Wall Plaza: *The "land for peace" process cannot possibly overcome the obstacle of this particular piece of land.*

very temporary structures that we lived in during our wanderings in the desert after the exodus from slavery in Egypt. But it's a much deeper message than that particular historical reflection. Indeed, the sukkah is a central assertion of the faith of Israel that God will stand with us in the most difficult situations when our very survival is threatened. The precarious sukkah represents the precarious nature of Israel's existence, a tiny state smaller in size than the American state of New Jersey. Surrounded as we are by enemies on all sides, the survival of Israel in the land of Israel is tied to our faithfulness to God, and to the covenant with the Almighty to protect the integrity of His chosen land and central in that divine connection is His chosen capital, Jerusalem.

Nevertheless, for David's sake, the Lord his God gave him a lamp in Jerusalem, to raise up his son (Solomon) after him, and to establish Jerusalem.

(1 Kings 15:4)

For from Zion shall come forth the Torah and the word of God from Jerusalem.

(Micah 4:2/Isaiah 2:3)

Jerusalem and the Temple Mount were the core issues that blew up the Camp David Summit because they symbolized, more than any other part of Israel, the real question of who the land of Israel really belongs to. There are many people in this world who believe in moral relativism, and therefore, they believe that these issues are not worth fighting over, but for the people of Israel almost across the political spectrum, the Old City of Jerusalem is central and symbolizes our very survival as a people. Yasser Arafat understood this and recognized that conceding on the core issue of Jerusalem would mean to abandon his dream of the destruction of Israel. This he was not willing to do, so the real barrier to a peace agreement was Arafat's inability to concede on this core issue and to end the conflict.

President Bill Clinton, looking to end his presidential career with a great success, seemed almost bitter about the failed summit and he placed the blame squarely on Arafat's shoulders, but he certainly wasn't the only one to do so.

Two books published in 2004 placed the blame for the failure of the summit on Arafat. They were *The Missing Peace* by longtime US Middle East envoy Dennis Ross and *My Life* by President Clinton. Clinton wrote that Arafat once complimented him by telling him, "You are a great man." Clinton responded, "I am not a great man. I am a failure, and you made me one."

During a lecture in Australia, Ross suggested that the reason for the failure was Arafat's unwillingness to sign a final deal with Israel that would close the door on any of the Palestinians' maximum demands, particularly the right of return. Ross claimed that what Arafat really wanted was "a one-state solution. Not independent, adjacent Israeli and Palestinian states, but a single Arab state encompassing all of historic Palestine."[17]

According to Foreign Minister Shlomo Ben-Ami, Israel tried to find a solution for Jerusalem that would be "a division in practice ... that didn't look like a division" – that is, Israel was willing to compromise on the issue, but needed a face-saving formula. The Palestinians, however, had no interest in helping the

Israelis; to the contrary, they wanted to humiliate them.

Nevertheless, Ben-Ami said Israel dropped its refusal to divide Jerusalem and accepted "full Palestinian sovereignty" on the Temple Mount and asked the Palestinians only to recognize that the site was also sacred to Jews. Arafat's response was to assert that no Jewish Temple had ever existed on the Temple Mount, only an obelisk; the real Temple existed in Nablus (Shechem). Not only did Arafat not make any accommodation to Israel, Ross said, "He denied the core of the Jewish faith." This stunning remark illustrated how Arafat had become caught up in the mythology he had created and indicated to the Americans that he was incapable of the psychological leap necessary – the one Anwar Sadat had made – to achieve peace.[18]

The events that followed the Camp David failure were even more revealing than the summit itself. After conceding nothing at Camp David, Arafat's triumphant return to celebration in the streets of Gaza and Ramallah was shocking to the Americans and the Israelis, who thought that the summit had ended in failure. What this proved, was that the residents of the Palestinian Authority stood with Arafat and his negotiating team in its refusal to accept that the Jewish people possess any rights in the Land of Israel. Despite the claims of Clinton and Ross that Arafat was the problem, the very fact that his unwillingness to compromise made him a hero in the PA controlled territories shows that the problem wasn't just Arafat, but that the problem went much deeper. Arafat's rejection of Jewish sovereignty in Jerusalem reflected the will of his real people, the Arab Muslim family of nations, who, despite public statements in English, still do not accept the existence of a Jewish state in the Middle East.

If the celebrations in the streets of Gaza and Ramallah had remained just an outward expression of moral support for their leader, there could have perhaps been a more successful follow-up to the second Camp David Summit, but this wasn't what ultimately happened. In fact, quite the opposite happened and it certainly wasn't accidental. The architects of the Camp David failure turned on the terrorist volume full-blast and the year 2000 became the year that the PA launched what became known as the Second Intifada, or the violent local uprising of terrorism against the Jewish state of Israel.

CHAPTER FOUR

Terror Works

We may hope for peace, but there is no goodness; for a time of healing, but behold, there is terror.

(Jeremiah 8:15)

J ust as much of President Bill Clinton's strategy for Camp David 2000 was based on President Jimmy Carter's successful strategy at Camp David 1978, the second intifada, which began in September of 2000, was birthed in the first intifada, which lasted from December 1987 to 1993 and was led by the Palestinian terrorist organizations. Each of these military organizations has always doubled as political movements, but the establishment of the Palestinian Authority surrounded them with an additional aura of credibility as they launched their Oslo-inspired terrorist war against Israeli civilians. Nonetheless, appearing to swallow the PLO propaganda in full, the mainstream media described each of these terror wars as a spontaneous grassroots reaction to Israeli "occupation". Yasser Arafat, claiming that he had no control over the "anger in the Palestinian street", watched "helplessly" for the next few years as the various terrorist organizations engaged in an intense and very violent competition to see who could launch the most attacks on Israelis, most of whom were innocent civilians.

The terrorism most certainly included Arafat's Fatah organization, as well as his al-Aqsa Martyrs' Brigade, often referred to as Fatah's military wing. The PLO Chairman and PA

So Happy Together (In Oslo): *Prime Minister Yitzchak Rabin stands together with Oslo architect Shimon Peres and PLO Chairman Yasser Arafat at the Nobel Peace Prize Ceremony in Oslo, Norway*

kingpin knew well how to change hats when the moment was right. As the proud father of modern terrorism who ironically had already received the Nobel Peace Prize for agreeing to the Oslo Accords, he could be a rabid hater of Jews one day and an honored guest in world capitals a day later.

Increasingly known to many by the lofty, respectable title of *Rais*, or President, Arafat wasn't bashful about using his world leader status as a cover for a cynical game of deception about his real intentions and goals. The idea was to fool the Western countries in order to protect him from the charge that as the head of the powerful Fatah, the dominant force in the PLO, he was the one who engineered the intifada, again proving his prowess as the master of double-speak. He alternately condemned the terrorist attacks in Hebrew and English, while in Arabic winking and expressing his approval of a massive wave of terrorism that lasted nearly a decade, killing 1,226 Israelis and wounding 8,342 just in the first seven years.[1]

Arafat's strategy, which enabled the continuous flow of European Union and American mega-dollars to the PA coffers, was no secret in the Arab world and was often explained in the Arabic media as an accepted form of public discourse with the Western media. There were in fact two medias – one that was privy to the truth and the other that would be lied to repeatedly and somehow accepted the abuse. The Palestinian leadership was remarkably adept at playing this game, but occasionally they slipped and let the cat out of the bag, thus revealing their true intentions:

It is the responsibility of the leadership to use it (the violent resistance and struggle) when it wants, in the proper place and at the proper time. I lived with Chairman Yasser Arafat for years. Arafat would condemn (terror) operations by day while at night he would do honorable things. I don't want to say any more about this.[2]

(Senior Fatah MP Muhammad Dahlan, July 2009)

Smile In English, Shoot In Arabic: *Fatah strongman Muhammad Dahlan (right) applauds PA President Mahmoud Abbas (2nd from right) and Prime Minister Ismail Haniyeh (2nd from left).*

The mouth of the righteous is a fountain of life, but the mouth of the wicked conceals violence.

(Proverbs 10:11)

The following excerpts from a 2002 Media Line news report reveals the two-faced public relations strategy used by the Palestinian leadership headed by Arafat. At least 18 Israelis, four of them children, were murdered in Arab terror attacks beginning with a post-Sabbath Saturday night bombing in a crowded Jerusalem neighborhood and continuing with terror strikes in Judea and Gaza:

> *The name of the shaheed (martyr) who carried out the operation was Muhammad Ahmad Darawna, announced Arafat's Voice of Palestine (VOP) in an almost celebratory manner, opening its Sunday morning (March 3) news broadcasts. It was referring to the man who blew himself up in Jerusalem, killing nine Israeli civilians, four of them children, Saturday night.*

It was one of the worst 12-hour periods of terror during the current Palestinian-Israeli war of attrition, and there was every sign that the violence would get worse as Yasser Arafat's Palestinian Authority signaled its strong support for the attacks on the Israelis.

The bomber's actions were greeted with a joyous street procession in the Duheishe Refugee Camp where he lived, as well as in the streets of Ramallah ... The PA declared Sunday "a day of solidarity with martyrs ..."

"An official statement" issued after midnight which was broadcast Sunday morning "condemned and condemns all terror against civilians," – an apparent attempt to curry favor with the Israeli Left and some Western governments who have insisted that Arafat stop and condemn terror.

But it was clear that the "official condemnation" was nothing more than lip service, because it once again refused to classify any Arab act as "terror" while specifically and repeatedly blaming the Israeli government for "its terroristic policies."

Throughout its Sunday morning broadcasts, VOP hosted speakers who spoke of "the Sharonite terror", "Sharon's terror", "the Zionist enemy", and "Zionist terrorism" – throwbacks to the Palestinian rhetoric before Israel and the Palestinians began signing agreements – collectively known as The Oslo Accords – in 1993.

A group of Palestinian snipers ambushed a convoy of Israeli soldiers and civilians early Sunday north of Jerusalem near the settlement of Ofra (in Samaria), killing at least eight, and wounding more than a dozen others, including rescue crews that attempted to take the wounded away in ambulances.

There were also two major attacks on convoys in the Gaza Strip and a major infiltration into Israel's Negev region – part of more than 50 serious Palestinian attacks in a 24-hour period.

The worst such attack, however, was when a Palestinian suicide bomber blew himself up Saturday night in the crowded Jerusalem neighborhood throwing himself on top of several families who had gathered together to celebrate the bar mitzvah of one of the children.

Flames from the blast engulfed nearby cars and buildings as the force of the blast was actually amplified by the crowded streets in the Beit Yisrael section of Jerusalem, a religious area where people tend to walk the streets leisurely after the Jewish Sabbath.

Nine people were killed, four of them children, and more than 60 were wounded in what the Voice of Palestine described less than two hours later as *"amaliyyat istish-had* – an operation of heroic martyrdom."

The Voice of Palestine also hinted strongly that the people in the neighborhood had, as it were, "gotten what they deserved" – a tactic it has used in the past to describe attacks on Jewish settlements:

> *This is a neighborhood that is full of extremist Jews.*
> (Muhammad Abd-Rabbo, the VOP Jerusalem reporter)

A man blew himself up next to a car in a neighborhood in which Jewish extremists reside.
(VOP anchorwoman Samah Masar in later broadcasts)

The use of the term "neighborhood full of extremist Jews" was similar to the Palestinian tactic after attacks on Jewish settlements when VOP customarily reminds listeners that the settlements were "built on land taken from our people." During those few weeks, Arafat's state-run Palestinian media had stopped even the pretense of condemning or criticizing even in English any attacks on Israeli civilians.

Not far from Arafat's headquarters in Ramallah, north of Jerusalem, large crowds of Palestinians celebrated the suicide attack in Jerusalem, and the statements and policies of Arafat's PA often seem indistinguishable from those of the Islamic terror groups – Hamas and Islamic Jihad.[3]

Terror means fear and there is no doubt that the new and intensified terror war created an atmosphere of fear on the roads and in the cities of Israel. "On the roads" referred mostly to the shooting attacks, ambushes, and sometimes infiltrations primarily in or near the communities (settlements) in Samaria and in Judea, otherwise known as the West Bank. "In the cities" referred mainly to the bus bombings, shooting sprees, and other attacks in the public spaces of the larger cities frequented by civilians, such as schools, cafes, and restaurants.

The purpose of terrorism is to terrorize. The only defense against terrorism is to refuse to be terrorized.[4]
(Author Salman Rushdie, November 1993)

While the above statement is perhaps an oversimplification of the issue, it comes from one who understands, on a personal level, what it is to be terrorized. Threatened with a fatwa, a death sentence, by the Ayatollahs of Iran in 1989 for expressing critical views about Islam in his book, he understood what it means to never know from where the next attack might come. The

Palestinian terrorist leadership directed their attacks primarily at those who couldn't defend themselves, a distinctly psychological approach that has long defined modern-day terrorism, reminding us of the strategy of Amalek, Israel's arch-enemy in biblical times, who would intentionally strike at those who were especially vulnerable, such as pregnant women, old people, and children:

> *Remember what Amalek did to you on the way, as you were leaving Egypt, that he came upon you on the way, and he struck those of you who were in the back, all the weaklings at your rear, when you were faint and exhausted, and he did not fear God.*
>
> (Deuteronomy 25:17-18)

When there is a wave of terrorist attacks in Israel, children are especially vulnerable. Constant terrorizing becomes an ongoing stressor and can devastate every part of their lives. This continual stress can cause their physical and emotional health to fail. Terrorized children often become susceptible to disease, mental issues, and anti-social behaviors.[5] However, it's important to make a distinction between feelings of fear and terror. Fear is a natural reaction to ongoing terrorist attacks, but it's not the same as being terrorized. One who is realistically afraid may have his life disrupted, but he or she can go on with the routines of life while taking precautions. On the other hand, a truly terrorized person totally loses the ability to function day-to-day. In this case, the terrorists have won, at least temporarily.

Israelis are a resilient people and are not known to cower under the threat of terrorism, i.e., to be terrorized, but realistic fear is certainly understandable. In the communities of Samaria and Judea that suffered a disproportionate degree of shooting attacks and terrorist infiltrations, especially in the first decade of the 21st century, realistic fear led to realistic, if surreal precautions. Aside from carrying guns for those who had them, there were many other preventative steps taken. Almost an entire fleet of public buses was armored and deployed for civilian use to help the residents to travel to work and school in the mornings and evenings. As for those who chose to or needed to travel to work in their private cars, many wore bullet-proof vests and even helmets. Others had metal caging installed on their windshields to protect against rock attacks. Still others carried fire extinguishers in their cars for quick response to firebomb attacks. These were just some of the defensive responses to the fear of terrorist attacks, but as bizarre as it felt to travel to work under such circumstances, it enabled people not to be terrorized, to go on with their daily routines, thereby stealing a portion of victory from the claws of the terror gangs of Fatah, the al-Aqsa Martyrs' Brigades, Hamas, and Islamic Jihad.

In the cities, the security checks became more stringent when boarding buses and entering bus terminals or stores and restaurants. As the risk of bus bombings in the major cities became greater, many people started to either take taxis more often or to walk more, while others completely avoided the most populated areas. Almost every restaurant or cafe had an armed guard checking those who entered, and those eateries that weren't equipped lost customers.

Despite the valiant efforts of Israel's citizens to maintain a semblance of normalcy, the terrorism took its bitter toll on the Israeli economy. For several years, the tourists nearly disappeared from the streets of central Jerusalem. Many of Jerusalem's hotels were eerily quiet and some were forced to rent out rooms well below market rates. In Judea and Samaria, the many history-rich tourist sites were bereft of visitors and some temporarily ceased to operate, such as the biblical site of Joshua's Tabernacle in Shiloh. After numerous murders on the roads, some in which both parents were shot and killed together, many couples stopped traveling in cars together so as not to turn their children into orphans.

For those of us living in Israel, the daily trauma of terror attacks on Israeli civilians, including women, children, and infants was a heart-wrenching state of affairs for all, but especially for those of us who either lost family members or were wounded ourselves. The trauma of terrorism can be healed, but those of us who have experienced it directly will tell you that it doesn't ever completely go away. It's up to us to take what the terrorists intended for evil and to turn it into good. We have an expression in Hebrew, "Hakol L'Tovah", which means, "Everything is for good." That doesn't mean that any terrorist attacks are good, but that everything happens for a good reason.

The Holocaust survivor and author Elie Wiesel wrote that one who has been through a trauma has a duty to tell the tale. I agree with that, but I also think that one who has experienced that trauma has the responsibility to take the horror and to turn it into good.

When my three-year-old son was shot in the head and I was shot in the leg by terrorists armed with AK 47 assault rifles, I didn't think of the good that could come from that horrible attack, but years later, having seen what the Shiloh Israel Children's Fund that I founded has done for the victims, I can see it in retrospect

Turning Darkness Into Light: *One of the main projects of the Shiloh Israel Children's Fund is the Therapeutic Horseback Riding program at the mountain horse farm in Shiloh. Children come for treatment from all over Samaria.*

Music For The Soul: *Children learn to express their emotions through music in order to overcome trauma, specifically the trauma of terrorism and war. The Shiloh Israel Children's Fund sustains the Therapy Center as well as subsidizing treatments for those in need.*

and I know how much good can come when we take the terrorists' evil intentions and create the opposite of what they had intended – thousands of emotionally and physically healthy children living and growing and rebuilding the biblical heartland of Israel.[6]

The Shiloh Israel Children's Fund is proud that it receives donations from thousands of people around the world who recognize the importance of standing with Israel in these difficult times.

That is what we can do as individuals, but to defeat the Islamic terrorism and to bring peace to the very troubled Middle East and to the world, we have to face the reality of the situation as it is and confront the evil head on. Yasser Arafat and his henchman were not benevolent, caring men of peace who were looking for a way to subdue a spontaneous popular rebellion in the streets against the so-called Israeli occupation. They were in fact the initiators, the catalysts, and the fanners of the flames, all rolled into one. Most of the world was left in the dark about the bitter truth that the Palestinian Authority heavily financed the terrorist organizations, as well as paying the terrorists and their families directly for carrying out the terrorist attacks on Israeli civilians.

Not wanting to burst the bubble of the sacrosanct peace process, most world leaders, as well as some Israelis who were heavily invested in the peace process, accepted the fictional distinction between the Palestinian Authority and the terrorist organizations that it sponsored, specifically Fatah, headed by none other than Yasser Arafat. Since it was no secret that Arafat wore three official hats – as Chairman of the PLO (the ideological/ political umbrella organization), the PA (the respectable, peacemaking government), and Fatah (the activist/terrorist organization) – it was necessary to create a fictional "independent" military wing in Fatah that would be like the wayward brother of Fatah that Arafat couldn't control. Thus, Fatah, which was really one organization under Arafat's leadership, came to be considered strictly an ideological organization with violent "splinters" like the Tanzim militia and the al-Aqsa Martyrs' Brigades. This protected Arafat and the PA leadership from the charge that they were engineering the terror war from above, but somehow the message didn't always reach the middle-tier al-Aqsa Martyrs' Brigades leaders:

> *The truth is, we are Fatah, but we didn't operate under the name of Fatah ... We are the armed wing of the organization. We receive our instructions from Fatah. Our commander is Yasser Arafat himself.*[7]
>
> (Leader of the al-Aqsa Martyrs' Brigades
> in PA autonomous Tulkarm in Samaria, March 2002)

In the backdrop of the failed peace process and the worst waves of terror in Israel's history, Israelis went to the polls in February of 2001, sending Ehud Barak to an early exit by handing a landslide victory to the Likud's fiery leader Ariel Sharon, who was known at the time for his aggressive promotion of Jewish settlement in the entire Land of Israel. Sharon came to office promising to put an end to the Palestinian terror war. His reputation as a no-nonsense warrior, as well as a human bulldozer, led people to hope and many to believe, that he would indeed get the job done. Sadly, this was not to be, and the attacks continued unabated.

On December 3, 2001, in reaction to a string of terrorist attacks, including bombings that killed 27 mostly young Israelis in a Jerusalem mall and on a Haifa bus, the Israeli Cabinet formally declared that the Palestinian Authority was "an entity supporting terrorism," a decision that a top government spokesman said justified military, political, and economic sanctions.[8]

As a result of this declaration, the Israeli government carried out a series of raids in the coming year in the PA autonomous areas. Some of these raids targeted the PA offices in Ramallah, and included putting Arafat under virtual house arrest in his headquarters, known as the Mukata. During these raids, the Israel Defense Forces (IDF) discovered a wealth of documents revealing the complicity of Arafat and the PA in encouraging and supporting terrorism. Some notable examples.

- On September 19, 2001, Arafat personally approved a request for payment of $600 to three people including Ra'ad Karmi, commander of the Tanzim in Tulkarm, who was personally involved in at least 25 shooting attacks against Israelis. Arafat funded Karmi even though Israel had placed Karmi on its "most-wanted" list just three months earlier. On the same day, Arafat approved payment to Amar Qadan, a member of his own Force-17 "Presidential Guard," who was involved in terrorist operations.

- A second request was faxed to Arafat to fund 12 more terrorists. According to Colonel Miri Eisin of the IDF Intelligence Branch, "Every single one of them was on our wanted list ... these are Tanzim members, which is Arafat's own party." Arafat knew well that these individuals were involved in terrorism. Nevertheless, on January 7, 2002, "Arafat himself – in his handwriting, with his signature ... agreed to pay the money."

- In a memorandum captured in Operation Defensive Shield (one of the largest IDF raids on the PA autonomous cities), the Secretary-General of the Fatah office in Tulkarm requested that Arafat provide $2,000 to each of 15 specifically named "Fighting Brethren" of the Tanzim military wing of Fatah. According to Israeli military sources, each of the "fighters" was involved in the **planning or execution of suicide attacks.** With his own signature in Arabic, Arafat authorized the payment of $800 to each of the "fighters" on April 5, 2001.

- On January 17, 2002, a Palestinian killed six Israelis and wounded twenty-six at a bat-mitzvah party in Hadera, initiated and planned by one of those on Arafat's gift list – Mansur Saleh Sharim, who was already responsible for the deaths of at least three Israelis. Senior Fatah figures in Israeli custody, like Marwan Barghouti, admitted subsequently that Arafat approved funding for Fatah operatives **with the knowledge that it would be used to finance terrorist attacks against Israeli civilians.**[9]

- In the early months of 2002, the number of attacks by the al-Aqsa Martyrs' Brigades, including suicide bombings, exceeded those of Hamas and Islamic Jihad. On September 16, 2001, the al-Aqsa Martyrs' Brigades requested payment to cover expenses for "production of explosive charges" from Arafat's financial confidante, Fuad Shubaki, who, as the head of the Palestinian Authority's "Armed Forces Financial Directorate," was also the mastermind behind the (enormous) Karine-A weapons ship delivery from Iran (intercepted by Israel at sea). That ship also carried huge amounts of C-4 explosives that could only be used for bombing attacks against Israel.[10]

- It should be noted that there were checkbooks of the PA's monthly salary account in the office of Marwan

Barghouti, the head of Fatah's "Supreme Movement Committee" in the West Bank. Barghouti or his aide-de-camp withdrew money in an authorized and systematic manner in order to finance Fatah branches in the West Bank. Barghouti was head of the Fatah/Tanzim in the West Bank and directed the murderous attacks of the al-Aqsa Martyrs' Brigades. He was arrested by Israel in April 2002 and remains in jail serving several life sentences.[11]

Furthermore, an in depth study of budgetary documents seized by the IDF from PA headquarters in Ramallah indicate that in the period of 2000-2001, between five and ten million dollars per month (!) were likely diverted from the PA Salary Budget alone to finance terror-related activities. As unveiled in the captured documents, the main methods utilized for this nefarious purpose which enabled the creation of surpluses in the PA salary account were the use of greatly different exchange rates than those that were reported to the (mostly European) donor nations, required payroll deductions to Fatah, and the integration of Fatah personnel in the PA salary payroll, despite their continued involvement in terrorism. The direct payments to the Fatah/Tanzim activists were in addition to these budgetary methods, and in accordance with the scope of attacks carried out by Fatah/Tanzim at any given point in the confrontation with Israel.[12]

All of the documents captured by the IDF in its raids clearly showed the full-fledged involvement and leadership of Arafat and his PA in leading the terror war against Israel. These examples of evidence given here are from a very small portion of the massive piles of incriminating documents captured by the IDF and common sense leads one to conclude that even the captured documents are only the tip of the iceberg, because the pattern continued well into the decade and right up to the present.

On November 11, 2004, Yasser Arafat was found dead. The official report from the Paris hospital said that he had died of a massive brain hemorrhage, but immediately the rumor mill got to work. Accusations abounded from the Arab world charging that he had been poisoned and that Israel was responsible. Other reports claimed that he had died of AIDS. Years later, two journalists for the left-wing Israeli newspaper Haaretz tried unsuccessfully to solve the mystery, but their research seemed to add more questions than it answered.

Here are some excerpts from their report:

While conducting research in 2005 for the second edition of our book "The Seventh War" (about the First Intifada), we got hold of the unabridged secret report on the death of the Palestinian president, compiled at Percy Hospital, in Paris where Arafat had been treated.

We held on to that report for the next few months and tried to decipher it, but it wasn't easy. First of all, the report was written in French, a language which is not our forte. Second of all, even after we brought the report to a translator, he told us that it was written in medical language, and in other words, we would need to find a French-Hebrew/English-speaking doctor.

After we found that, we started to crack the report. This was a hundred-page document full of contradictions and questions.

For instance, the report mentions that samples of Arafat's blood taken while he was still in Ramallah and sent to a lab in Tunis had disappeared. We're not talking about blood samples from some John Smith or Moishe Moishe, but Yasser Arafat – and they just disappeared.

Another example: Yasser Arafat's personal doctor, Ashraf al-Kourdi, who was only sent over to Arafat on October 27 (two weeks and a day after the Palestinian leader fell ill) told us then, as we were conducting our research, that he knew that the AIDS virus had been found in Arafat's blood during tests at Percy. The report doesn't mention this. But the report also does not mention a single word about Arafat being tested for AIDS, even though he had some of the symptoms common in AIDS patients. Al-Kourdi claimed at the time that it was Israel's Mossad that infected Arafat's blood with the virus.[13]

However, as reported in World News Daily, there are some who have claimed that Arafat may have acquired AIDS by the serial sexual abuse of children. James J. Welsh, who in the early 1970s monitored communications for the National Security Agency, related to Arafat's Fatah movement, said:

One of the things we looked for when we were intercepting Fatah communications were messages about Ashbal (Lion cub) members who would be called to Beirut from bases outside of Beirut. The Ashbal were often orphaned or abandoned boys who were brought into the organization, ostensibly to train for later entry into Fedayeen fighter units. Arafat always had several of these 13-15 year old boys in his entourage. We figured out that he would often recall several of these boys to Beirut just before he would leave for a trip outside Lebanon. It proved to be a good indicator of Arafat's travel plans. While Arafat did have a regular security detail, many of those thought to be security personnel – the teenage boys – were actually there for other purposes.

Ion Pacepa, who was deputy chief of Romanian foreign intelligence under the Ceausescu regime and who defected to the West in 1978, says in his memoirs the Romanian government bugged Arafat and had recordings of the Arab leader in orgies with his security detail.

Various Israeli security sources have in the past claimed Arafat's former personal driver – a Mossad double agent – used to find teenage boys to bring back to the PLO leader. His wife, Suha, mostly lived abroad and rarely saw her husband.[14]

Arafat's unusual relationship with his wife and possible sexual abuse of young boys aside, it was also explicitly pointed out that Suha refused to let the doctors conduct a liver biopsy in his final days, but no explanation was given as to the reasons. The Haaretz report related to the repeated charge that Israel poisoned Arafat:

> *Every senior Palestinian official interviewed in the investigation claimed that Israel poisoned Arafat. This claim requires special examination, of course, because of the political implications. Nevertheless, everyone we spoke to on the Israeli side has vehemently denied the accusations. Not with a smile, nor even with half of a smile. Everybody, without exception, claimed that this was complete nonsense.*

With all these accusations, we must remember that in November 2004, there was no Israeli interest in killing Arafat, who, by the way, was isolated, weak, and in many ways, irrelevant. In addition, a former Israeli official emphasized that the Israeli government had promised the American administration not to turn him into a *shaheed*.

Toxicity tests conducted on Arafat in Paris brought up nothing. The report itself shows the results of blood tests taken from Etienne Louvet, sent to the toxicity lab of the Paris Police and the military hospital. Etienne Louvet was the code name that the doctors used whenever they sent Arafat's blood tests, in order to keep the results of the tests secret.

The report mentions the names of the different poisons they tried to pinpoint (in order to find poison, it's necessary to look for it specifically) – but Polonium 210, the poison discovered in an Al Jazeera investigation, wasn't on the list at the French lab."[15]

The one important issue perhaps not emphasized enough in these reports was the obvious interest of the Arab world in showing Israeli complicity in the death of Arafat, and therefore, the trumpeting of the poisoning theory. To this day, the mystery of Arafat's death hasn't been solved, but the disappearing blood samples and missing information in the report, along with the contradictions in the various statements certainly added to the intrigue and the questions about the life and death of this charismatic individual.

In any event, Arafat's longtime deputy Mahmoud Abbas assumed the leadership of the PA, stepping into the very large shoes of a legend, and quickly found himself the recipient of Prime Minister Ariel Sharon's unexpected generosity in a strange turn of events in which Israel had decided to unilaterally withdraw entirely from the Gaza region along the southwestern Mediterranean coastline. Dubbed the Disengagement, the withdrawal from Gaza was very controversial in Israel and a major trauma for the social fabric of the Jewish state. This territory, one of those that had been captured from Egypt in the Six Day War of 1967, was the site of a thriving bloc of idealistic Jewish communities, the heart of them known as Gush Katif, or the Harvest bloc, known for their agricultural creativity and innovation.

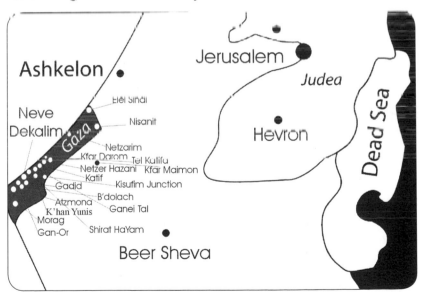

A Thriving Bloc Of Idealistic Communities: *The Jewish communities in the Gaza Strip, adjacent to the large cities of Ashkelon and Beer Sheva. Since the Israeli withdrawal from Gaza, those cities have become prime targets of Hamas missiles fired from the locations where children once played.*

A dream of 30 years...

...destroyed in a few moments

Before And Immediately After The Destruction – Gush Katif, 2005: *The destruction of the Jewish communities in Gaza and their eventual replacement by Hamas missile launching pads is one of the great lessons in modern Israeli history. A similar withdrawal from the hills of Samaria, which has been considered by Israel's political echelon, would bring a torrent of missiles raining down on Ben Gurion International Airport.*

At PA insistence, Sharon added several Jewish communities in northern Samaria to the list of those to be evacuated and destroyed. All in all, a total of 10,000 peaceful, law-abiding Jews were evicted from their homes in a surreal, yet major military operation for which the army trained for months. Synagogues were destroyed. Homes and playgrounds were demolished, as were the internationally acclaimed Gush Katif greenhouses. To this day, many of the former residents remain homeless. The entire operation was engineered by the former celebrated general turned prime minister, Ariel Sharon, who insisted at the time that, in the absence of serious peace

Expelled 10,000 Jews: *In a shocking betrayal of those who had elected him, Prime Minister Ariel Sharon adopted the unilateral withdrawal plan of his soundly defeated opponent. The result was 10,000 homeless Jews and years of terrorist missile attacks on Israeli cities and towns.*

negotiations, the withdrawal would ultimately bring peace, but for now it would bring real security and international acceptance to Israel. His basic argument was that when the international community would see how much Israel was willing to concede for peace, they would cease to view the tiny nation as a stubborn, intransigent pariah state. Furthermore, the Jewish communities of Gaza had suffered many terrorist attacks emanating from the large populations in the adjacent Arab cities. Sharon argued that once we removed the vastly outnumbered Jewish communities from Gaza, an unnecessary irritant would be removed from the equation, thereby improving the atmosphere.[16]

Looking back years later, most Israelis recognize that none of Sharon's predictions came to fruition. As soon as the last Israeli left Gaza and the bulldozers had destroyed the last Israeli home, the terrorist organizations, in particular the Hamas, jumped in to fill the void, setting up military bases and missile-launching sites on the land where there once were greenhouses, playgrounds, nurseries, and schools. In the succeeding years, many thousands of Hamas and Islamic Jihad missiles have been launched at Israel's cities from Gaza, forcing the IDF to reenter Gaza to destroy the launching pads and bomb factories on several occasions, including the December 2008 – January 2009 operation in which Israel responded to hundreds of rockets and mortars that had been fired at Israeli cities and towns for several weeks by sending its soldiers into Gaza en masse. As of 2013, the Israeli-abandoned areas have continued to be used as missile launching pads in a bizarre turning of good into evil. Did Sharon really expect something different to occur or was it all politics? We may never know.

On the PA political front, things heated up as well, and this only heightened the tensions with Israel. There were elections in the Palestinian Authority-controlled territories in January of 2006, in which the Hamas won a decisive victory, capturing 76 of the 132 parliamentary seats, giving the party officially at war with Israel the right to form the next cabinet under the Palestinian Authority's president, Mahmoud Abbas, the leader of Fatah, which won just 43 seats in a shocking show of weakness for Abbas.[17] The two terrorist powers have been at odds and struggling for power ever since, causing a split in the PA, with Hamas seizing absolute control of Gaza and Fatah, deeply concerned about the rise in Hamas' popularity besieging the Hamas in Judea and Samaria. Meanwhile Abbas has been clinging to power, postponing elections for PA president and parliament several times as Hamas' popularity continues to grow.

An obvious question that needs to be asked is why a former champion of the settlement enterprise such as Ariel Sharon would launch a unilateral withdrawal from Gaza, thereby unleashing the inevitable maelstrom of events that has led to the untenable state of affairs that Israel finds itself in less than a decade later. After all, this was the same Ariel Sharon that had stated several years earlier – prior to announcement of the disengagement plan – that "the fate of (Gaza Jewish community) Netzarim will be the fate of Tel Aviv."[18] How does one explain such a zig-zag from defender and patron of the settlements to their chief prosecutor?

When attempting to explain the inexplicable behavior of politicians, we are often led to the deeply immoral, but all too human crime of corruption. Exactly one day before Sharon had a massive stroke and collapsed into many years of coma, police investigators announced to the press that they had found evidence of a three million dollar bribe that Sharon allegedly had received from one of the major international investors in the Palestinian Authority's Jericho Casino.[19]

During the period leading up to the Disengagement, there had been scathing reports of alleged shady dealings, which seem to explain Sharon's abrupt change from active supporter of settlement to active destroyer.

Perhaps we will never know the full truth, and there certainly are those who still have an interest in burying the allegations, but it appears to many, that personal corruption may have been a major motivating factor in the tragic decisions of Israel's leaders to carry out the great destruction.

Journalists Raviv Druker and Ofer Shelach, authors of the Hebrew book, *Boomerang*,[20] claimed that in late 2003, there was no ready plan for evacuating Gaza unilaterally, certainly not one that Sharon was supporting, but there was growing despondency over a spike in Arab-Israeli violence and the looming corruption investigation that threatened both Sharon and his son Gilad, a businessman who worked for the suspected bribe-giver. The authors reported that a closed meeting of Sharon's top advisors was held at the Sharon Ranch in the Negev desert to find a way to get the corruption story off the front pages. One participant suggested starting a war, but that suggestion was quickly rejected. In the end, the Gaza disengagement plan was adopted as a way for Sharon to create new, positive headline spin and to ingratiate him with the left-leaning media. It seemed to have been a successful strategy, as the corruption news quickly faded from the media until after the full expulsion from Gaza and northern Samaria had been completed.

Through justice a king establishes a land, but a man of graft tears it down.

(Proverbs 29:4)

Interestingly, Gilad Sharon now claims that he was the one who hatched the idea of the disengagement from Gaza.[21] Given the sordid background of corruption that the authors described in their book, it certainly does not come as a surprise.

Whatever the reasons, the flight from Gaza did occur, with much sadness, but with minimal resistance. No doubt the leadership of the Palestinian Authority was watching the Israelis' tormented evacuation with much excitement and even amusement, as they were handed the entire Gaza region on a silver platter, with absolutely no concessions required on their part.

You make of us an object of strife unto our neighbors, and our enemies laugh amongst themselves.

(Psalms 80:7)

The Palestinians quickly and gleefully adapted to the new strategic advantage that Sharon had given them and the terror war continued, while taking on a modified form, using their new geographic, military assets to focus more on air offensives on the southern cities of Israel in the Negev desert and extending outward from there.

Despite the new focus on missile attacks, the PA's structural support network for the terror war remained basically the same and was even expanded under the leadership of Mahmoud Abbas. However, despite the continued focus on encouraging terrorism, Abbas brought a noticeably different image to the world of peacemaking and terrorism. Always impeccably dressed in a suit and tie, Abbas was in many ways the polar opposite of his mentor Arafat, who was always unshaven and dressed in militia garb. Soft-spoken and lacking the charismatic fire of an Arafat, Abbas was nonetheless a hard-core Fatah ideologue who was not willing to compromise on principles, even if he was prepared to smile, to shake hands with Israelis, and to make conciliatory statements about peace, in English of course, but with no concessions of any kind. Abbas was born in 1935 in the city of Tsfat (Safed) in Israel's Galilee region. He fled to Syria with his family during the 1948 Arab-Israeli War. Abbas graduated from the University of Damascus before going to Egypt where he studied law. Abbas later entered graduate studies at the Patrice Lumumba University in Moscow, where he earned a Candidate of Sciences degree (the Soviet equivalent of a PhD). The theme of his doctoral dissertation was "The Other Side: the Secret Relationship Between Nazism and Zionism", revealing a passion for a Holocaust revisionism that sharply contradicted his conciliatory image.[22]

Abbas came into conflict with Palestinian militant groups, notably the Palestinian Islamic Jihad Movement and Hamas because his "pragmatic policies" were opposed to their hard-line approach. However, he made it clear that he was forced to abandon, for the moment, the use of arms against Israeli civilians inside the green line due to its ineffectiveness.[23] In other words, if the situation would change and they would become more effective politically, he would happily authorize attacks in the heart of Tel Aviv, but in any event, attacks in Judea, in Samaria, and in much of Jerusalem were okay and even praiseworthy in his eyes. Abbas quickly became a welcome figure in western capitals, mainly due his moderate image. The problem was that it was only an image and the two-faced nature of Arafat gradually become apparent in the case of Abbas, who was more respected in the eyes of the world as a moderate, but was no less supportive of violent activities.

The financing of terrorism both inside and outside the 1967 borders continued under Abbas and was even formalized. In April 2011, a new PA law was enacted authorizing payment of monthly salaries to all Palestinian and Israeli-Arabs who were being imprisoned for terrorist crimes in Israeli prisons. In other words, car thieves would not receive a payment, just those imprisoned for violent terrorist actions, such as murders, bombings, shootings, and stabbings.[24]

Furthermore, liberal justice-seekers need not fear – the Palestinian Authority is an equal opportunity employer. The PA's Ministry for Prisoner Affairs stated that its policy has always been to pay salaries to prisoners and their families "regardless of their political affiliations."[25] The simple meaning of this is very straightforward – despite Abbas's personal preference for Fatah, when it comes to aiding terrorists, there are no distinctions made between Fatah, Tanzim, al-Aqsa Martyrs' Brigades, Hamas, Islamic Jihad, al-Qaeda, and any other terrorist organizations. All are worthy and all receive.

As of May 2011, the PA was distributing a total of over five million dollars monthly to terrorist prisoners, a figure similar to the amounts distributed by the PA under Arafat's leadership.[26] The key difference was that now it was all legal under the PA's morally convoluted system of laws.

How do we explain this? Yes, individuals like Abbas certainly look like respectable, moderate individuals. This brings to mind Bashar Assad of Syria, who came to power in the backdrop of his father's death and ruled with an iron fist much like his father, until civil war broke out in Syria, when Sunni Muslim rebels decided that they would try to overthrow him. With a British wife of Syrian heritage and a Western education, many naive American politicians reached out to him and pandered to him as a computer-literate, university-educated reformer.

We came in friendship, hope, and determined that the road to Damascus is a road to peace.[27]
(House Speaker Nancy Pelosi, April 4, 2007)

Western educated, western tailored individuals like these may appear more appealing to those in the West than a costumed Muammar Gaddafi, but the cover image doesn't make the book friendly, nor does it make it reasonable.

The real question that needs to be asked is this: What is it in

Coming In Friendship: *US House of Representatives Speaker Nancy Pelosi visits President Bashar Assad in Damascus, Syria. Western leaders have long made the tragic mistake of thinking that computer skills and good knowledge of English is synonymous with a fondness for Western values.*

the Arab or Islamic culture that leads to a widespread passion for, and at least acquiescence to the rampant terrorism that permeates the Islamic world, with the support of so many of the Islamic leaders? The degree of support doesn't seem to correlate with whether the leader is an elected leader, a dictator, or a monarch. The level of support or at least tolerance for terrorist organizations remains strong. How do we explain it?

CHAPTER FIVE

Irreconcilable Differences

Is there a reason that the heralded peace process has not even come close to people's expectations?

Does such an idealized, much promoted, and financed process actually fail in a vacuum?

Is it more complex than that?

Obviously, a singular opportunity to advance the peace process has appeared, and we must not miss it. This window of opportunity that has opened to us is made of glass and must be handled with care.[1]

(Shimon Peres, September 2007)

The politicians, some of whom have staked their reputations on the achievement of peace, or at least on the vision thereof, often talk about the peace process as if we are parrots repeating the same catch-all phrases over and over. They declare that we now have – a singular opportunity, a window of opportunity, an opportune moment, and that the time has never been better for peace – all of these mantras are recited ad nauseum by politicians and journalists, without much thought given to the incongruous nature of such statements when compared to the present realities. The unpleasant truth is that Israel and its neighbors are coming from very different places and that the chance of peace at present is virtually nil. Without examining the respective philosophies of life and death that guide our conflicting cultures, we can't hope to understand why world leaders, master negotiators, and acclaimed peace-makers have all failed to bring a lasting peace between Israel and the other countries in the Middle East.

Even if it doesn't jibe well with the golden calf worship of the peace process trumpeters, a more honest appraisal of the difficulties in the said process demands that we examine the cultural differences that have repeatedly thrown seemingly intractable obstacles in the path of the peace negotiators, at every turn and at every juncture, not to mention at every summit.

> *Love your neighbor as yourself.*
>
> (Leviticus 19:18)

> *Hillel says, Be like the disciples of Aaron – Love peace and pursue peace. Love all living things and bring them closer to Torah.*
>
> (Mishna: Ethics of the Fathers 1:12)

> *I shall terrorize the infidels. So wound their bodies and incapacitate them because they oppose Allah and his apostle.*
>
> (Muhammad, Sura 8:12)

> *Allah's apostle said, You (the Muslims) will fight with the Jews until some of them will hide behind stones. The stones will (betray them), saying, O Abdullah (slave of Allah), there is a Jew hiding behind me; so kill him.*
>
> (Hadith Sahih Bukhari 4:52:176
> Narrated Abdullah bin Umar)

A Sura is a chapter of the Koran, while the Hadith is the Islamic oral tradition based on the teachings of Muhammad, but the contrast between those texts and the biblical/Jewish texts are glaring. Judaism, the national religion of Israel, established some 4000 years ago with its universal mission of spreading love and goodness, has long been a beacon of light to the world. It also provided the moral basis of Western civilization, particularly in the United States of America. Furthermore, it's obvious that without Judaism, there would have been no Christianity, since Christianity evolved over the years from the teachings of a Jew in the Land of Israel, known then by the Hebrew name of Yeshua, known now to the world as Jesus. He was born in Bethlehem in Judea, in the area that much of the world calls the West Bank. While Christians and Jews certainly have some theological differences, both religions are clearly rooted in the Hebrew Bible.

It's true that there are verses in the Hebrew Bible that call for Israel to take very aggressive, violent actions in specific contexts, such as against Israel's arch-enemy Amalek, who intentionally targeted women, children, and the elderly. However, it never calls for Jihad, or holy war, as Islam does, against "the unbelievers," meaning those who simply don't believe in the teachings of Islam. According to Torah, the status as an enemy is based on evil actions, not beliefs. The Islamic intolerance of those with differing beliefs leads to the terrorism, riots, and even wars, all of which we have seen in Islamic abundance in modern times.

Jihad is not just an option for a Muslim, but is considered to be the highest obligation of a Muslim. Let's examine some sources from a high school curriculum, not from radicals like the Iranian Ayatollahs, but from what is considered to be a Western-friendly moderate nation, whose king an American president bowed down to not so long ago.[2]

> *In these verses is a call for Jihad, which is the pinnacle of Islam. In (Jihad) is life for the body; thus it is one of the most important causes of outward life. Only through force and victory over the enemies is there security and repose. Within martyrdom in the path of Allah (exalted and glorified is He) is a type of noble life-force that is not diminished by fear or poverty.[3]*
>
> (From the Twelfth Grade
> Saudi Arabian School Curriculum, 2008)

Honoring The King: *President Barack Obama breaks protocol and raises many eyebrows and questions by very publicly bowing down to King Abdullah of Saudi Arabia. This was especially odd for an American president, since Saudi Arabia teaches its children the praiseworthiness of Jihad and hatred of Jews, Christians, and all other non-believers.*

We need to be clear here about the true meaning of martyrdom in the Islamic mindset. We are not speaking about a Gandhi-like peaceful protest that just happens to end in death, nor are we speaking about a hunger strike. In Islamic parlance, martyrdom denotes a fight to the death against the infidels.

In its general usage, Jihad is divided into the following (two) categories:

> *Wrestling with the infidels by calling them to the faith and battling against them.*[4]

(From the Twelfth Grade
Saudi Arabian School Curriculum, 2008)

When the Islamic sources, such as the Koran (the Islamic "Bible") or the Hadith (orally transmitted teachings of Islam's founder, Muhammad) speak of the enemy, they are usually, but not exclusively, referring to Jews and Christians:

> *As cited in Ibn Abbas: The apes are Jews, the people of the Sabbath; while the swine are Christians, the infidels of the communion of Jesus.*[5]
> (From the Eighth Grade
> Saudi Arabian School Curriculum, 2008)

> *The Jews and Christians are enemies of the believers, and they cannot approve of Muslims.*[6]
> (From the Ninth Grade
> Saudi Arabian School Curriculum, 2008)

This "us against them" mentality is rooted in the founding of Islam in the Arabian Peninsula 1,400 years ago. The founder of the religion was Muhammad, who was born in the year 570 of the Common Era (CE) into the Quraysh tribe – the ruling tribe in Mecca – in the Arabian Peninsula, what is now called Saudi Arabia.[7] Muhammad is believed to have been a direct descendant of Ishmael (a belief that he was quite proud of), the wayward son of the biblical figure Abraham and his maidservant Hagar. Abraham is, of course, well known as the founder of Monotheism and Judaism. Ishmael was the controversial progenitor of the (now almost exclusively Muslim) Arab nation.[8]

> *And he (Ishmael) will be a wild man; his hand will be against everyone and (therefore) everyone's hand will be against him ...*
> (Genesis 16:12)

Muhammad was born into a very difficult family situation; psychologists would surely concur that his tragic and topsy-turvy upbringing undoubtedly affected his ability to relate to others throughout his life.

Muhammad's father, Abd Allah, passed away six months

before Muhammad was born and his mother, Amina, died when he was just six years old. After her death, he was left in the care of his grandfather, Abd al-Muttalib, who died two years later. From then on, Muhammad was raised by his uncle Abu Talib, a textile merchant who often traveled with his nephew on cross-country camel caravans. It was on these travels that young Muhammad learned about different cultures and religions. As he was illiterate, this wealth of knowledge was acquired solely by listening to stories and oral traditions about Judaism, Christianity, Zoroastrianism, and the various Arabian pagan religions that were prevalent at the time.

Beginning in 610 CE, at age 40, Mohammed tried to convert those who came to worship Mecca's 360 different pagan gods. Though hoping his faith would be embraced by Jews, Christians, Zoroastrians and Pagans, as it had elements of each, he only converted around 150 of them. His initial "Meccan" verses had been "revealed" to him while in Mecca.

These "weak" verses were actually respectful of Christians and Jews:[9]

If you are in doubt about the revelation I am giving you ask those who read the Bible before you.

(Sura 10:94)

There is no compulsion in religion.

(Sura 2:256)

The trouble started in earnest when Muhammad's claims of prophecy were rejected by the Jews, Christians, and pagan Arabs in Mecca and he fled to Medina, also on the Arabian Peninsula, where he sought to acquire new followers, officially establishing Islam in the year 622 CE. Muhammad's response to this rejection, which made this angry young man even angrier, was the creation of a new angry, intolerant god whom he called Allah, and new angry verses, the Medina verses, which became the continuation and indeed, the core of Islam. These new verses advocated compulsion, ruthlessness, and hatred of Jews and

Christians, often referred to as the infidels, and of any non-Muslims. What is often referred to today as "radical Islam" or "Islamism" is actually the post-Mecca phase of Islam, which has clearly become the dominant force in Islam today.

Unlike their spiritual leader, some of Muhammad's followers were literate, and began to write down his sayings and stories. These narratives eventually evolved into the writings of the Koran, divided into 114 Sura (chapters), as well as the Hadith, the written version of the Islamic oral tradition, the instructions of how to lead a proper life, according to the teachings of Muhammad.[10] Muhammad is revered as the Sunna, or the example of how to behave, and therefore, when he called for Jihad against the unbelievers, or single-handedly beheaded 700-800 Jews in one day, or engaged in submissive relationships with his 31 wives and assorted other sexual partners (some as young as nine years old), the Muslim faithful respond with similar malignant behavior and justify it by pointing to the (similarly abusive) behavior of Muhammad.

> *Aisha said, The Apostle of Allah married me when I was seven years old. (The narrator Suleiman said: Or six years.) He had intercourse with me when I was nine years old.*
>
> (Hadith Sunan Abu Dawud, Volume 2:2116)

In the United States, these are the crimes of statutory rape and, at the very least, sexual harassment. However, in the rose-colored world of political correctness, harsh criticism of Islam is considered to be Islamophobia, which is really just a term designed to prevent people from honestly examining the issues. The politically-correct mob tells us that we need to try to understand such behavior through the prism of respect for Islamic mores and cultural differences. In modern newspeak, one might say that Muhammad was a charismatic leader, but a flawed individual who perhaps stretched the boundaries of what was acceptable. If we adhere to the premise that truth is subjective and/or relative, then we need to be respectful of the cultural uniqueness in the Muslim world that enabled such behavior, because we shouldn't unfairly judge him according to westernized social norms.

On the other hand, however, if we have the courage to examine such behavior objectively, we perceive a mentally sick and abusive individual who used his spiritual, physical, and political position of authority to take advantage of young girls. In essence, his position of importance served his megalomania and hedonistic lifestyle at the expense of those who were powerless to object. If a Jewish or Christian spiritual leader today behaved in such a manner – and we have certainly seen such unfortunate examples – he would not only be lambasted through the media, condemned, and removed from his pulpit or position, but he would possibly be arrested for statutory rape and/or sexual harassment. And he would deserve it.[11]

Although polygamy was (and still is) permitted in Islam, the Koran (Sura 4:3) officially limited men to four wives. Nonetheless, Muslims are allowed by the Koran to have an unlimited number of concubines and can have sex with women their right hands possess (Sura 23:5-6, Sura 33:50, Sura 7:29-30). Muhammad's teachings and example provided the justification for this religiously-sanctioned abuse of women, which has become the model behavior for observant Muslims to emulate. Even married women were to submit to the abuse of their husbands and often this abuse could be physical, as well as psychological:

Men are the protectors and maintainers of women, because Allah has given the one more (strength) than the other, and because they support them from their means. Therefore the righteous women are devoutly obedient, and guard in (the husband's) absence what Allah would have them guard. As to those women on whose part you fear disloyalty and ill-conduct, admonish them (first), (next), refuse to share their beds (and last) beat them (lightly) ...

(Sura 4:34)

Any objective person can see that Muhammad considered women to be playthings who existed to satiate his own hedonism and to enable him to abuse his position of power. Shockingly, his abusive behavior is described in some detail and praised in Muslim sources. What is particularly troubling is that the idea of repentance is conspicuously absent from any discussion of Muhammad's abuse of power. This is in sharp contrast to the punishments meted out for any misguided behavior of leaders in the Bible, as well as the emphasis on their need to repent – to admit their mistakes and to correct them in the future. The verses in the Koran justify and even seem to give a divine stamp of approval for Muhammad's much more frequent abuses, which once again remind us of Muhammad's forefather, Ishmael, not just his violent nature, but the sexually perverse and abusive behavior. We read in the Bible that Abraham's wife, Sarah, had been unable to bear children, and that she gave Abraham the go-ahead to have a child with the servant, Hagar. However, as the child Ishmael reached adulthood, his problematic behavior had to be dealt with.

> *And Sarah saw the son of Hagar the Egyptian woman playing. So she said to Abraham, Drive out this slave woman with her son, for the son of that slave woman shall not inherit with my son, with Isaac!*
>
> (Genesis 21:9-10)

The Jewish source of wisdom, the Midrash, teaches a lesson about Ishmael and Islam from the original Hebrew by the great Torah sage, Rabbi Akiva, who, in his uniquely concise style, hits the nail on the head:

> *Rabbi Akiva expounded ... Playing (in this context) can only mean sexual sin ... This teaches that Sarah would see Ishmael breach garden fences, hunting down men's wives and raping them.*
>
> (Genesis Rabah 53:11)

> *Ten measures of sexual sin descended to the world –*
> *Arabia took nine.*
>
> (Talmud, Kiddushin 49b)

There are commentaries in the Talmud that define the word *playing* as murder, while in this context, it refers to something else, and we see that just as Muslims follow the ways of Muhammad, the founder had a well-known role model of his own. The extent to which Muhammad was influenced by his progenitor Ishmael is open for debate. What is not debatable, however, is that although many centuries have passed since the days when Muhammad *played,* there is no doubt that his freewheeling, no-limits lifestyle is imitated and legitimized by those who revere his memory, as well as his behavior.[12] For example, in Shiite Muslim society, there is a phenomenon called pleasure marriages, which is basically a form of legalized and religiously sanctioned prostitution. The following report describes its resurgence in the new, democratic Iraq:

> *In the days when it could land him in jail, Rahim al-Zaidi would whisper details of his muta'a only to his closest confidants and the occasional cousin. Never to his wife.*
>
> *Al-Zaidi hopes to soon finalize his third muta'a, or pleasure marriage, with a green-eyed neighbor. This time, he talks about it openly and with obvious relish. Even so, he says, he probably still won't tell his wife.*

The 1,400-year-old practice of muta'a – ecstasy in Arabic – is as old as Islam itself. It was permitted by the prophet Muhammad as a way to ensure a respectable means of income for widowed women.

Pleasure marriages were outlawed under Saddam Hussein but have begun to flourish again. The contracts, lasting anywhere from one hour to 10 years, generally stipulate that the man will pay the woman in exchange for sexual intimacy. Now some

Iraqi clerics and women's rights activists are complaining that the contracts have become less a mechanism for taking care of widows than an outlet for male sexual desires.

Most Shiite scholars today consider it halal, or religiously legal.[13] These cases of legalized and religiously-sanctioned prostitution are only the tip of the iceberg, in a torrent of cases of violent and/or psychologically coercive sexual and physical abuse of young girls, grown women, and yes, even sexual enslavement of young boys[14] in the Islamic world, particularly in countries like Afghanistan.

> *A spring there, called Salsabîl. And round about them will (serve) boys of everlasting youth.*
>
> (Sura 76:18-19)

Indeed, we know that similar behavior exists in Western civilization, but the key difference is that in the Islamic world, it's religiously-sanctioned, and therefore legitimized, as evidenced by the numerous sources in the Koran/Hadith, backed up by many Islamic scholars to this day, who support such abusive crimes as child marriages in countries like "moderate" Saudi Arabia.[15] What is bizarre is that because Muhammad is revered by Muslims around the world as "the prophet", and because any criticism of his behavior often results in threats or actual cases of violence against the critics, the world sits in fear and doesn't speak out. The liberals, the feminists, and the child's rights defenders, who usually are passionate advocates of their views, are all strangely silent to the plight of women and children in the Islamic world.

As we discussed earlier, Muhammad is the Sunna, the example to be followed by all observant Muslims. And why would they criticize Jihad when the Sunna advocated violence against those who disagree?

> *Allah's Apostle said, I have been ordered to fight with the people till they say, None has the right to be worshipped but Allah ...*
>
> (Hadith 4:196 Narrated Abu Huraira)

Soon after his initial consolidation of power on the Arabian Peninsula, Muhammad, having intimidated and violently suppressed any opposition, took his battle to the next phase, which was forced conversion to Islam. Thus, after a society had suffered an initial conquest, and the normal orgy of slaughter, rape, and enslavement had subsided, what Muhammad called "the surrender of the tongue" might be made "available" to the survivors. This referred to sparing lives of the conquered if they would give lip service as to becoming Muslims. Muhammad well knew that with the destruction of all churches, synagogues, and temples, combined with forced instruction in the Koran for children of the conquered societies and a death sentence for backsliders, subsequent generations of the conquered territories would be Muslim.[16]

As you can see, Islam has a strange attitude towards tolerance and freedom of thought. The Islamic way stands in stark contrast to free speech and free religion as enshrined in the respected First Amendment to the US Constitution, the document that to this day defines more than any other, the meaning of freedom in the modern world, but the Islamic world lives by a very different standard:

> *Fight those who believe not in Allah nor the Last Day, nor hold that forbidden which hath been forbidden by Allah and His Messenger, nor acknowledge the Religion of Truth, from among the People of the Book, until they pay the Jisyah (Poll Tax) with willing submission, and feel themselves subdued.*
>
> (Sura 9:29)

> *Remember thy Lord inspired the Angels with the message: I am with you: give firmness to the Believers: I will instill terror into the hearts of the unbelievers: Smite ye above their necks and smite all their fingertips off them.*
>
> (Sura 8:12)

As we discussed earlier, there are those Muslims who identify two definitions for Jihad, or holy war. The first is the struggle or war against what they call the unbelievers. This is of course an unacceptable contradiction of the tolerance that has come to be the norm in Western civilization. For that reason, many Islamic scholars in the United States and elsewhere tend to downplay the violent, intolerant side of Islam, as we see in this segment of an essay by one apologist for Islam:

"The literal meaning of Jihad is 'to strive.' More importantly, it means to progress in all aspects of one's life. Although the word Jihad is used by the Western media with militant connotations, in truth, it covers a vast range of human activity, such as family life, work, spiritual development, and justified military defense."[17]

For those accepting the sanitized Muslim "party line" that Jihad doesn't really mean holy war against the unbelievers, here are some more recent quotes of prominent "Westernized" Muslims:

Islam must rule the world and until Islam does rule the world we will continue to sacrifice our lives.[18]

(Mustaq Aksari,
a spokesman for Al-Badr,
a subversive Islamic movement still active
in the United States – on CNN
September 19, 2001, just eight days after 9/11)

A decree of death has been passed on America. The judgment of God has been rendered, and she must be destroyed.[19]

(Nation of Islam leader
Louis Farrakhan in Harlem, 1997)

Islam isn't in America to be equal to any other faith, but to become dominant. The Koran should be the highest authority in America, and Islam the only accepted religion on Earth.[20]

(Omar Ahmed, Chairman of the Board
of CAIR – The Council of American Islamic
Relations – ostensibly a civil rights organization, July 1998)

The fanaticism of those Westernized Muslim leaders doesn't sound very different than the leader of the Islamic Revolution in Iran:

Islam makes it incumbent on all adult males, provided they are not disabled or incapacitated, to prepare themselves for the conquest of other countries so that the writ of Islam is obeyed in every country in the world.[21]

(Ayatollah Khomeini,
the Muslim cleric
and hero of the Islamic Revolution in Iran)

Let there be no illusions. The State of Israel is a critical first down in the football game of Islamic world domination, but we are not the end goal. Nuclear Europe is next as the Islamic tsunami of demography, now with a growing 15-25% in many major European cities continues to exploit liberal guilt and pursues the educational and legal changes that will make Sharia a reality within a generation. For those still unaware, Sharia is the oppressive Islamic law that is the basis for the legal system in almost every Islamic country. An imposition of Sharia would most likely include the following changes and deviations from current systems of law in the West:

- There would be no religious freedom. Islam would be the only religion permitted and infidels would be subject to severe punishment, including death.
- Muslim leaders would command offensive, aggressive and unjust Jihads.
- Unmarried fornicators would be whipped and adulterers stoned to death.
- Husbands would be allowed to hit their wives, even if the husband merely fears aggressiveness from his wife.

- Homosexuals would be executed.
- Critics of Muhammad, the Koran and even Sharia would be put to death.
- Highway robbers would be crucified or mutilated.
- An injured plaintiff would be allowed to exact legal revenge, physical eye for physical eye.
- As punishment, a thief's hand would be cut off, regardless of whether the thief was male or female.
- Drinkers and gamblers would be whipped.[22]

The Islamic ideologues have made Sharia inroads in Europe, but they haven't hid the reality that their eventual target is none other than the United States of America. Yes, the so-called Great Satan is the ultimate touchdown, so to speak.

There are two primary groups of Muslims in the world, the Sunnis, as represented mainly by countries like Saudi Arabia, Egypt, and Jordan, countries that have long been considered to be the moderate peace-makers, as opposed to the Shiite Muslims, fiercely and vocally anti-American and anti-Israeli, the leadership of which has long been based in Iran. Some self-proclaimed Middle East experts have perpetuated this inaccurate portrayal of the Islamic world, but the reality is quite different. Yes, there is rivalry between the two groups, often resulting in death and destruction, but the cases of quiet cooperation between the terrorist groups from both camps are more frequent. Particularly worrisome is the coordination between the Sunni Muslim Hamas terrorist organization and the Shiite Muslim Hezbollah, an ongoing cooperation that somehow transcends the Shiite-Sunni animosity.

This report from Reuters:

A Hamas Web site disclosed on Wednesday that fighters from the Palestinian militant group had received funding and training from the Iranian-backed Hezbollah movement in Lebanon, a link long denied by Hamas leaders.

Jihadists United For The Cause: *In recent years, there has been a strengthening of the alliance of Sunni Hamas and Shiite Hezbollah terrorists. In this photo, newly sworn-in Hezbollah "Fighters for Gaza" salute during a 2009 ceremony in Lebanon. The ceremony was attended by Hamas leader in Lebanon Osama Hamdan.*

A Hamas spokesman in Gaza declined to comment on the information on the website, run by the group's armed wing, Izz el-Deen al-Qassam. There was no immediate comment from Hezbollah in Beirut. The site said Hamas, which is dedicated to Israel's destruction and won the January 25 Palestinian election, received funds from Hezbollah to set up the first Hamas cell in the occupied West Bank after an uprising began in 2000.

Over the course of three years, members of the cell – 10 of whom were eventually killed or jailed by Israeli security forces – carried out attacks that killed 18 Israelis.

Hamas member Jaser al-Barghouthi, who formed the cell and recruited its gunmen, sent emissaries to Lebanon "to be trained by Hezbollah and return with needed funds," the website said, without giving a figure.[23]

This cooperation has continued into the succeeding years, as we can see from this 2011 sub-headline:

Hamas says Hezbollah sent it report in 2006 detailing how to broker exchange deal with Israel; Hamas briefs Gaza groups on details of deal.[24]

Washington believes that Hezbollah and Hamas are helping their backers in Iran to expand its influence in Yemen at the expense of Yemen's Gulf neighbors, the US envoy to Sanaa told pan-Arab daily Al-Hayat on Sunday.

In a London interview, Gerald Feierstein was quoted as accusing Hezbollah and Hamas of helping their backers in Shi'ite Iran at the expense of the Gulf Cooperation Council (GCC) ...[25]

On September 12, 2012, it was reported that one of Hamas's most senior leaders, Mahmoud al-Zahar, met with Hezbollah head Hassan Nasrallah. The two met in Lebanon, according to the Lebanese daily Al-Ahbar. The two reportedly talked for six hours about ties between their respective terrorist groups.[26]

The fervor for Jihad inevitably brings us back to Israel and Jerusalem, for what other way is there to prove the supremacy of Allah than to disinherit the Jews, the chosen people, from the Land that many millions of people assert was given to Israel by God? This is a passion that is eagerly pursued to varying degrees by virtually all of the Islamic nations and terrorist organizations. After all, isn't killing Jews consistent with Islamic teachings? As you will see from these first two quotes, Christians certainly aren't spared. However, the special venom is reserved for the Jews:

And thou seest (Jews and Christians) vying one with

another in sin and transgression and their devouring of illicit gain. Verily evil is what they do. Why do not the rabbis and the priests forbid their evil speaking and their devouring of illicit gain? ... Evil is their handiwork.

(Sura 5:62-63)

Fight against such of those (Jews and Christians) ... until they pay for the tribute readily, being brought low.

(Sura 9:29)

Allah fighteth against them (the Jews). How perverse they are!

(Sura 9.30)

They (the Jews) are the heirs of Hell ... They will spare no pains to corrupt you. They desire nothing but your ruin. Their hatred is clear from what they say ... When evil befalls you they rejoice.

(Sura 111:117-120)

Those who disbelieve our revelations, we shall expose them to the fire. As often as their skins are consumed, we shall exchange them for fresh skins that they may taste the torment.

(Sura 4:56)

It isn't some new religion called "Radical Islam" or "Islamism" that we are talking about. This is core Islamic teaching that comes straight from the Koran and the Hadith and doesn't leave much room for other interpretations, unless one disputes the validity of the Koran and the Hadith, which most intellectually honest Muslims would be afraid to do. They would rather not expose their lives to violent threats from their Muslim brethren.

Whoever changes his Islamic religion, kill him.
(Hadith Sahih al-Bukhari 9:57)

And therefore, few Muslim voices of opposition are heard against the bigoted words of hatred, as they continue to teach hatred of the Jew in the mosques around the world, at times careful to keep the focus on Israel, as if the respective hatred of the Jews and of Israel is not one and the same. They may refer in public to the "Zionist enemy" without using the word "Jew", but the message of bigotry and hatred remains clear – No Jews allowed.

If it were simply a Nazi-like belief system, it would be bad enough, but that vile hatred is being used to support and legitimize a very strange revision of history – to deny the several thousand year connection of Israel to Zion (the Land of Israel).

> *The oppressor will not last in Jerusalem; the oppression will not endure. Victory will come, Allah willing. This land is Allah's best land, for which he chooses the finest of his believers, as it is written in the words of the Prophet (Muhammad).*[27]
>
> (Mahmoud Abbas, PA President,
> as reported in Al-Hayat Al-Jadida, July 11, 2010)

> *We have frankly said, and always will say: If there is an independent Palestinian state with Jerusalem as its capital, we won't agree to the presence of one Israeli in it.*[28]
>
> (Mahmoud Abbas, PA President,
> to reporters in Ramallah, December 2010).

> *(Jerusalem has been) throughout history, the capital of the Palestinian state and the capital of the Palestinian people.*[29]
>
> (Mahmoud al-Habbash, Abbas's Minister of Religion,
> PA TV (Fatah), August 20, 2010)

Obviously, neither claim is correct. There has never been a Palestinian state and Jerusalem was never the capital of an

Arab or Muslim state. Nonetheless, the PA minister warned there would be religious war over Jerusalem:

> *The term "war" cannot be erased from the lexicon of this region as long as Jerusalem is occupied.[30]*
>
> (PA TV (Fatah), August 20, 2010)

This brings us back to the core symptom of contention – Jerusalem. I refer to it as a symptom because it is merely a reflection of the deeper issue, the inability of the Islamic culture to countenance Jewish sovereignty over the Land of Israel or of any territory in the Middle East. Yet due to its deeply spiritual nature and contentious religious history, the very mention of Jerusalem conjures up images of high priests and prophets, crusaders and caliphates. Jerusalem is almost a magical word and even its sudden absence from the political discourse creates controversy and gets everyone's attention, as we saw during the height of the 2012 US Presidential campaign.

During the 2012 Democratic National Convention (DNC) in the United States, a furor arose when it was discovered that the words "God" and "Jerusalem" (as the capital of Israel) had quietly been omitted from the Democratic platform after having been included in the 2004 and 2008 platforms. The ensuing ruckus over the significance of the omission and concern over the resultant votes that would be lost in the upcoming presidential and congressional elections caused the chairman of the Democratic National Committee to call for a quick voice vote on the convention floor to reinstate the two words into the platform. After the motion was met with vocal resentment, DNC chairman Antonio Villaraigosa had to call the vote three times to reinstate language into their party platform that recognizes Jerusalem as the capital of Israel as well as the words "God-given" in a passage about employment. Even after he declared the vote affirmative, he was roundly booed for pushing the motion through.[31]

Needless to say, the omission of Algiers or Buenos Aires

from the platform wouldn't have caused such a commotion. The reinsertion was not surprising due to the potential loss of support that could result from such a glaring omission in the platform of a president who already was perceived by many as anti-Israel. Case in point: President Obama's first phone call to a foreign leader as president was to PA President Mahmoud Abbas, his first two high-profile visits overseas were Islam-pandering tours to Turkey and to Egypt, while in his four years as president, he didn't visit Israel even once, but had a series of high-profile run-ins with Israeli Prime Minister Benjamin Netanyahu, even once abruptly leaving him alone in the White House to fend for his dinner with his aides. No, the omission from the platform didn't surprise me, but it saddened me, knowing that it came from the party of Harry Truman, who was strongly biblically connected and became deeply emotional any time he met an

Biblically Connected And Emotional About Israel: *President Harry Truman (left) receives a menorah (candelabra) in thanks for his support for the reestablishment of the State of Israel from Israeli Prime Minister David Ben-Gurion (right) and Foreign Minister Abba Eban.*

Israeli leader.[32]

When Chief Rabbi Yitzchak Isaac HaLevi Herzog of the newly established state of Israel came to visit President Truman in early 1949, the two had a very moving exchange, in which the Rabbi expressed his thanks to the President for his recognition of Israel.

He then went on to say the following words to the president:

God put you in your mother's womb so that you could be the instrument to bring about the rebirth of Israel (as a sovereign nation) after almost two thousand years.

Truman was visibly moved. Herzog then opened his Bible, and with the President reading along in his own Bible, the Rabbi read from the Book of Ezra (1:2), in which the Persian King Cyrus spoke the following words:

The Lord, God of Heaven has given me all the kindness of the earth; and he has commanded me to build Him a house (Temple) at Jerusalem, which is in Judah.

On hearing these words, Truman rose from his chair and with great emotion, tears glistening in his eyes, he turned to the Chief Rabbi and asked him if his actions for the sake of the Jewish people were indeed to be interpreted thus and (that) the hand of the Almighty was in the matter. The Chief Rabbi reassured him that he had been given the task once fulfilled by the mighty King of Persia, and that he too, like Cyrus, would occupy a place of honor in the annals of the Jewish people.[33]

To stand with the Jewish people, with Israel, and with Jerusalem, was an idea that Harry Truman knew well, but it derived from the biblical roots of that relationship, which of course is connected to God.

Founders of the United States, like Benjamin Franklin and Thomas Jefferson, had a passion for biblical Israel that Truman obviously shared, but these individuals would have appeared awfully out of place at a Democratic Convention that didn't see

A Culture Built On Biblical Foundations: *The early American leaders, like founding father Benjamin Franklin, were biblically-literate, and therefore, understood that the road to blessings and success went through the values and heritage of, and their connection with, the people of Israel.*

fit to include God and Jerusalem in its platform, but seemed more concerned with highlighting LGBT (Lesbian Gay Bisexual Transsexual) rights than the historic bond between Israel and the United States.

The American obsession with the goal of a Palestinian state, which had intensified during the Obama years and which by all accounts would insist on having its Palestinian capital in Jerusalem, has clearly made a DNC assertion of Jerusalem as the eternal capital of Israel an uncomfortable proposition. Nonetheless, there can be no more vacillating. We are approaching a breaking point and stands will have to be taken. It's not possible to stand with Israel and to support a terror-breeding Palestinian state, not in the biblical heartland of Israel and certainly not in any part of Jerusalem.

The canard that one can be pro-Israel and pro-Fatah or pro-Hamas at the same time is a falsehood that shouldn't be given the light of day, for it is by nature a refutation of Israel's roots as the biblical nation.

One cannot honestly demand that Israel hand over Shiloh, where Samuel the Prophet grew up into prophecy and be respectful of Israel's roots.

One cannot honestly demand that Israel hand over Bethlehem, where King David lived (and where Jesus was born) and still be respectful of Israel's roots.

Finally, one cannot possibly demand that Israel surrender the Temple Mount in Jerusalem, where the two Holy Temples stood, while still claiming to be pro-Israel.

An Israel without its roots would be an Israel with no justification, no legal or moral claim for its existence. Any organization or individual that claims to be pro-Israel must be biblically-consistent, i.e, respectful of Israel's biblical heritage, for an Israel that abandons its biblical heritage is like a tree without roots or a building without a foundation. It would die a slow death or would simply collapse.

CHAPTER SIX

Deception On All Levels

P ublic denial of the Holocaust is considered by many to be one of the most heinous thought crimes, worthy of imprisonment in some countries. The intentional slaughter of six million Jews and many others by Adolf Hitler and his Nazi war machine in Europe was a horrific event unrivaled in world history, and therefore, its very denial is considered to be a crime in countries in which free speech is paramount. But isn't this a paradox? Isn't it contradictory to place limitations on freedom of thought short of an outright call for violence?

Having grown up in the United States, a country which epitomizes free speech perhaps more than any place in the world, I have always seen red lights flashing when freedom seems to be restricted by governing authorities. Nonetheless, many countries have considered Holocaust revisionism to be beyond the bounds of free speech, because the Nazi strategy exploited free speech in order to undo those very same freedoms that they exploited to come to power.

In our time, we are being faced with a serious dilemma from a different source, from a different ideology that uses many of the same revisionist tools that the Nazis used in their rise to power. What is a free society to do when it is confronted by a force and/or an ideology that doesn't respect the entire concept of free thought yet exploits it to distort history and restrict freedom?

In Islam, there is a concept called *taqiyya*, which means deception, which is permissible in order to further the cause of Islam and it generally refers to relationships with the unbelievers, or non-Muslims. There are two forms of lying to unbelievers that are actually religiously sanctioned under certain circumstances, "taqiyya" (saying something that isn't true – outright lying) and "kitman" (lying by omission). The circumstances are typically those that are believed to advance the cause of Islam – in some cases by gaining the trust of non-believers in order to draw out their vulnerability and defeat them. Here are seven examples of deception or lying that Muslims follow and use to justify their own religiously flavored lying:

1.   Muhammad signed a 10-year treaty with the Meccans that allowed him access to their city while he secretly prepared his own forces for a takeover. The unsuspecting residents were conquered in easy fashion after he broke the treaty two years later, and some of the people in the city who had trusted him at his word were executed.

2.   Muhammad used deception to trick his personal enemies into letting down their guard and exposing themselves to slaughter by pretending to seek peace. This happened in the case of Kaab Ibn al-Ashraf and again later against Usayr ibn Zarim, a surviving leader of the Banu Nadir tribe, which had been evicted from their home in Medina by the Muslims. At the time, Usayr ibn Zarim was attempting to gather an armed force against the Muslims from among a tribe allied with the Quraish (against which Muhammad had already declared war). Muhammad's "emissaries" went to ibn Zarim and persuaded him to leave his safe haven on the pretext of meeting with the prophet of Islam in Medina to discuss peace. Once vulnerable, the leader and his thirty companions were massacred by the

Muslims with ease, belying the probability that they were mostly unarmed, having been given a guarantee of safe passage (Ibn Ishaq 981).

3. Leaders in the Arab world routinely say one thing to English-speaking audiences and then something entirely different to their own people in Arabic. Yasser Arafat was famous for telling Western newspapers about his desire for peace with Israel, then turning right around and whipping Palestinians into a hateful and violent frenzy against Jews.

4. The 9/11 hijackers practiced deception by going into bars and drinking alcohol, thus throwing off potential suspicion that they were fundamentalists plotting Jihad. This effort worked so well, in fact, that even weeks after 9/11, John Walsh, the host of a popular American television show, said that their bar trips were evidence of "hypocrisy."

5. The transmission from Flight 93 records the hijackers telling their doomed passengers that there is "a bomb on board" but that everyone will "be safe" as long as "their demands are met." Obviously none of these things were true, but these men, who were so intensely devoted to Islam that they were willing to "slay and be slain for the cause of Allah" (as the Koran puts it) saw nothing wrong with employing taqiyya in order to facilitate their mission of mass murder.

6. The Islamic Society of North America (ISNA) insists that it *"has not now or ever been involved with the Muslim Brotherhood, or supported any covert, illegal, or terrorist activity or organization."* In fact, it was created by the Muslim Brotherhood and has bankrolled Hamas. At least nine founders or board members of ISNA have been accused by prosecutors of supporting terrorism.

7.   Prior to engineering several deadly terror plots, such as the Fort Hood massacre and the attempt to blow up a Detroit-bound airliner, American cleric Anwar al-Awlaki was regularly sought out by (media networks) NPR, PBS and even government leaders to expound on the peaceful nature of Islam.[1]

The cavalier use of lying in the Islamic world certainly calls into question the reliability of peace treaties and the trustworthiness of the peace partners. All of Israel's peace negotiations with the Muslim nations or organizations have been based on the belief that once a treaty is signed, it will be adhered to, but the Islamic concept of taqiyya seems to get in the way of sincere peace negotiations, especially when the precedent is to use negotiations for strategic advantage, not for peace.

> *The Palestinians have no interest whatsoever in establishing peace, the pathway to peace is almost unthinkable to accomplish ... I look at the Palestinians not wanting to see peace anyway, for political purposes, committed to the destruction and elimination of Israel, and these thorny issues (of precarious borders and security), and I say, There's just no way.*[2]

(US Presidential Candidate Mitt Romney, May 17, 2012)

The result of the Oslo Accords was to weaken Israel by arming terrorist "policemen" in the Palestinian autonomous areas and to encourage massive foreign assistance to the Palestinian Authority for the cause of peace and economic development, money that was used to arm their assorted terrorist organizations. It was a bold strategic move for the Palestinian leadership to pretend sincerity when speaking in English, Hebrew, and assorted other non-Arabic tongues, and to go forward with the peace process, in order to strengthen their political, their economic, and their military position for the battles to come.

The sixth president of the United States, John Quincy Adams, had a lot to say about Islamic deception, mainly due

Treachery And Violence Taught As Principles Of Religion: *US President John Quincy Adams understood and denounced the deceptive nature of Islam, without fear of being called "Islamophobic".*

to his involvement in conflicts with the Barbary Pirates, among other Islamic variations (the terrorist organizations of their time), who were terrorizing American ships at sea and demanding substantial indemnity (tribute or payment), which was an outright monetary bribe, to guarantee safe passage. Muslim ransoms varied from $300 for a seaman to $1,000 for a captain. Tripoli offered a short-term peace for $66,000 plus commissions and a long-term peace for $160,000 plus commissions. Similar tributes were demanded by other Muslim nations, totaling $1.3 million, enormous sums of money at that time. Paying a tribute, though, did not guarantee peace.[3]

This was what President Adams had to say about Muslim treaties:

> *The victorious may be appeased by a false and delusive promise of peace and the faithful follower of the "prophet" may submit to the imperious necessities of defeat, but the command to propagate the Moslem creed by the sword is always obligatory when it can be made effective.*

> *The commands of the prophet may be performed alike, by fraud or by force. Of Mahometan good faith, we have had memorable examples ourselves:*

> *When our gallant Commodore Stephen Decatur had chastised the pirate of Algiers, till he was ready to renounce his claim of tribute from the United States, he*

signed a treaty to that effect: but the treaty was drawn up in the Arabic language, as well as in our own; and our negotiators, unacquainted with the language of the Koran, signed the copies of the treaty, in both languages, not imagining that there was any difference between them.

Within a year the Dey (Omar Bashaw) demands, under penalty (threat) of the renewal of the war, an indemnity in money for the frigate taken by Decatur; our Consul demands the foundation of this pretension; and the Arabic copy of the treaty, signed by himself is produced, with an article stipulating the indemnity, foisted into it, in direct opposition to the treaty as it had been concluded. The arrival of Commodore Isaac Chauncey, with a squadron before Algiers, silenced the fraudulent claim of the Dey, and he signed a new treaty in which it was abandoned; but he disdained to conceal his intentions; My power, said he, has been wrested from my hands; draw ye the treaty at your pleasure, and I will sign it; but beware of the moment, when I shall recover my power, for with that moment, your treaty shall be waste paper.

He avowed what they always practiced, and would without scruple have practiced himself. Such is the spirit, which governs the hearts of men, to whom treachery and violence are taught as principles of religion.[4]
(John Quincy Adams, "Essays on Turks", pp. 274-275)

The strategy of making a treaty in order to refuel and rebuild armaments and then scrapping the treaty once strong enough to defeat the enemy militarily comes from the Sunna himself (Muhammad, the Islamic model for proper behavior), as explained by noted historian William Federer:

The Muslim concept for treaty is "Hudna", which means cease-fire, (generally to last for ten years, based on the precedent of the Treaty of Hudaybiyyah between Muhammad and the Quraysh tribe).[5]

Mohammed set the example that when Muslim armies are weak, they should seek truces and when they are strong, they should fight without mercy. Kaab Ibn al-Ashraf was a member of the Jewish tribe, Banu al-Nudair.

It was reported that Kaab had supported the Quraishites in their battle against Mohammed.

Mohammed was also infuriated because he heard Kaab had recited amorous poetry to Muslim women. Mohammed asked for volunteers to rid him of Kaab Ibn al-Ashraf, saying Kaab had harmed Allah and His Apostle (meaning himself).[6]

When Kaab Ibn al-Ashraf was preparing to fight Mohammed, his tribe was strong and it was not easy to gain access to him. Mohammed granted permission for his warrior, Ibn Muslima, to lie in order to infiltrate Kaab's camp and murder him. Ibn Muslima went to Kaab, saying he was no longer loyal to Mohammed, thus gaining Kaab's trust. Ibn Muslima said he wanted to talk privately and lured Kaab away from his other soldiers, then murdered him under cover of darkness.[7]

Winston Churchill described this as a "system of ethics, which regards treachery and violence as virtues rather than vices."[8]

Following in the ways of the Sunna, there are many recent examples of this lethal use of deception. One of the most notable was the Fort Hood Massacre.

On November 5, 2009, a fundamentalist Muslim, Major Nidal Malik Hasan killed 13 people and wounded 28 people at the largest US Army base, Fort Hood, TX. This event had roots in the Islamic tradition of deception (since Hassan had pretended to be a loyal American soldier). It was later discovered that this was a man whose professional business card said on it *SOA (SWT)*, which means Soldier of Allah – literally translated: Glorious

No Fondness For Islam: *In his 1899 book, "The River War", British statesman Winston Churchill was very critical of the Islamic penchant for lying and violence, as well as perverse sensuality, and abuse of women.*

and exalted is Allah.[9] It has also been reported that Hassan had ongoing correspondence and consultation with an American-Muslim *imam* (religious leader/scholar). According to his website, this imam, named Anwar al-Awlaki, previously served in Denver, San Diego and Falls Church, Virginia. Al-Awlaki had also benefited from the American educational system, having achieved a degree in civil engineering from Colorado State University and a master's degree in educational leadership from San Diego State University.

After the attack at Fort Hood, al-Awlaki, who reportedly had been giving ongoing advice to Hassan, wrote the following commentary on his blog:

> *Nidal Hassan is a hero. He is a man of conscience who could not bear living the contradiction of being a Muslim and serving in an army that is fighting against his own people. Any decent Muslim cannot live, understanding properly his duties towards his Creator and his fellow Muslims, and yet serve as a US soldier. The US is leading the war*

Soldier Of Allah: *US Major Nidal Malik Hassan massacred 13 people and wounded 28 people at the largest US Army base, Fort Hood, TX. His Islamic-American mentor called him "an American hero."*

*against terrorism which in reality is a war against Islam.
Its army is directly invading two Muslim countries and
indirectly occupying the rest through its stooges.*[10]

Al-Awlaki's father, Nasser al-Awlaki, was also a beneficiary
of Western higher education, receiving a master's degree in
agricultural economics from New Mexico State University in
1971 and a doctorate at the University of Nebraska. The family
returned to Yemen in 1978, where Nasser served as Agriculture
Minister and as President of Sanaa University. He lived the
American immigrant dream of academic achievement so that
his son could become a real American, but his Islamic doctrine
of deception dictated otherwise. He pretended to be a loyal
American so he could undermine and eventually destroy the
country that welcomed him in.

Speaking on CNN, the elder al-Awlaki pleaded his son's
case, proclaiming:

*He has been wrongly accused, it's unbelievable. He
lived his life in America, he's an all-American boy. My
son would love to go back to America, he used to have a
good life in America. Now he's hiding in the mountains,
he doesn't even have safe water to drink.*[11]

Such is the plight of the *all-American boy* who apparently
was an important source of inspiration for another *all-American
boy*, Major Nidal Hassan. But were these really all-American
boys? Obviously they were simply following the religious
precept of taqiyya, or deception to further the cause of Islam,
pretending to be loyal Americans while in reality being fervently
loyal to an ideology that was, is, and always will be hostile to
American values. The frightening reality appears to be that
Hassan, who shouted the Islamic war cry *allahu Akhbar* (Allah
is greater) before shooting his victims, was himself a Muslim
terrorist in American army uniform and that this horrific act of
terrorism was enabled by America's blindness to taqiyya.

The deception in diplomacy that Islam's founder

Muhammad encouraged and that President John Quincy Adams so poignantly deplored has always been present in the Islamic rewriting of history, especially when it pertains to the history of Israel.

At the second Camp David Summit in 2000, it was clear to all that Jerusalem would be central to the resolution or dissolution of the summit. Unlike past negotiations that avoided the issue, then Prime Minister Ehud Barak was determined to confront the issue for good or for bad and he was willing to go a long way towards compromise, to such an extent that there was an uproar in much of the Jewish world when word started to leak out about aspects of the Israeli proposals, such as the willingness to give up Israeli sovereignty on the Temple Mount, the holiest site in Judaism. After all, it is called the Temple Mount for a reason. This was the place where the two Holy Temples of Israel had stood for hundreds of years, after having been purchased by King David of Israel specifically for that purpose years earlier:

> *And when Araunah looked out, he saw the king and his servants coming towards him; and Araunah went forth, and did obeisance to the king with his face to the ground.*
>
> *And Araunah said, Why has my lord the king come to his servant?*
>
> *David said, To buy the threshing floor of you, in order to build an altar to the Lord, that the plague may be averted from the people.*
>
> *But Araunah said to David, Let my lord the king take and offer up what seems good to him; here are the oxen for the burnt offering, and the threshing sledges and the yokes of the oxen for the wood. All this, O king, Araunah gives to the king. And Araunah said to the king, The Lord your God accept your (offerings).*

But the king said to Araunah, No, I will buy it from you for a price; I will not offer burnt offerings to the Lord my God which cost me nothing.

So David bought the threshing floor and the oxen for money – fifty shekels.

David built there an altar to the Lord, and offered burnt offerings and peace offerings. So the Lord answered the prayers for the land, and the plague was averted from Israel.

(II Samuel 24:20-25)

The purchase was made by King David, but it was his son King Solomon who would direct and oversee the actual building of the Temple on the Temple Mount in Jerusalem:

Now Hiram, king of Tyre, sent his servants to Solomon, when he heard that they had anointed him king in place of his father; for Hiram always loved David.

And Solomon sent word to Hiram, You know that David my father could not build a house for the Name of the Lord his God because of the warfare with which his enemies surrounded him, until the Lord put them under the soles of his feet. But now the Lord my God has given me rest on every side; there is neither adversary nor misfortune. And so I propose to build a house for the Name of the Lord my God, as the Lord said to David my father, Your son, whom I will set upon your throne in your place, shall build the house for My Name.

(I Kings 5:1-5)

In the four hundred and eightieth year after the Children of Israel's exodus from the land of Egypt in the fourth year of Solomon's reign over Israel, in the month of Ziv (Iyar), which is the second month – he built the Temple for God.

(Kings 6:1)

Retaining Wall Of "The Alleged Temple": *People often make the mistake of thinking that the Western Wall is the holiest site in Judaism. That distinction rests with the Temple Mount that it helps to support. Nonetheless, even the history of the Western Wall has been distorted by Palestinian revisionists.*

As we clearly see from the historical record, the Temple stood on the Temple Mount in the Old City of (now eastern) Jerusalem, and that it was built under the direction of King Solomon on land that was legally purchased by his father and predecessor, King David. There is no doubt that both father and son would have been greatly perturbed, to say the least, to know that some 3,000 years later, there would be a people calling themselves the Palestinians, a name that hadn't yet been coined by the Romans, who hadn't yet conquered Jerusalem or destroyed the Temple, but that these Palestinians would be engaging in particularly pernicious historical revisionism denying this central period in Israel's history.

(The) purpose is to achieve its black goals: Destroying

*the al-Aqsa Mosque, building the "alleged Temple,"
taking over the Muslim and Christian holy sites, and
destroying its (Jerusalem's) institutions in order to empty
it, uproot its residents, and continue its occupation and
Judaization.*[12]

(PA President Mahmoud Abbas, WAFA, August 21, 2012)

*There will be no peace, security, or stability unless
the occupation (Israel), its settlements and settlers will
be evacuated from our holy city and the eternal capital
of our state.*[13]

(PA President Mahmoud Abbas,
Al-Hayat Al-Jadida, August 22, 2012)

Abbas's statement also said that all of Israel's archeological digs and tunnels ... will not change the reality of the city ... and will not create a (Jewish) right based on what he called fantasy and legends.

What fantasy and legends was he referring to? The answer is clear from his use of the expression the "alleged Temple".

The research group Palestinian Media Watch checked its archives and found that the official PA press reported the use of the expression "alleged Temple" at least 97 times by heads of the PA, its institutions and its media, just in 2011 and 2012. This number refers only to the use of this term. The PA has denied Jewish history in Israel and Jerusalem hundreds of times as part of its official policy of revisionist history, and has also fabricated an ancient Palestinian history in the land, thereby contradicting the accepted theological premise that says that only God can create something from nothing.[14]

This ongoing distortion of history, carried out with no shame in front of the eyes of the world, is scandalous and causes biblically-literate and historically-literate people to scratch their heads, as well as quite a few archeologists. Nonetheless, the historical revisionists in the PA and their cohorts throughout the Islamic world continue their cynical game of religiously-sanctioned lying to further the cause of Islam.

The media cultivation of Abbas's image as a reasonable moderate has continued unabated for years. This is the same Abbas who, on a visit to Bethlehem, publicly held up a stone model of the map of "Palestine" that erases Israel.[15]

If we want to put the Islamic concept of taqiyya and its use in the exploitation of the Middle East conflict into its proper context, we need to understand that there is a dangerous collusion going on today between the far secular Left and the Islamic ideologues, both of which have deep roots in the use of deception to further their disparate goals. While most Israeli politicians would be hesitant to admit it publicly, it is indeed the shifting alliances on the world stage that are affecting the Middle East and paramount among them is the above-mentioned alliance, which though usually unofficial, is fueling the Islamic tsunami that is storming its way across the Middle East and is creeping its way through Europe and yes, even beginning to make serious inroads in North America.

In order to understand the collusion between these two, we need first to understand that there is a commonality of interests joining them together. One might logically guess that there could be no alliance between two parties that have such vastly divergent worldviews and long-term goals. The far Left desires a one-world government or a communist government that would take from the rich and give to the poor, while supporting revolutionary movements around the world in the spirit of Mao Zedong, Joseph Stalin, Che Guevara, and Fidel Castro. On the other hand, the Islamist leadership wants a caliphate, a world totally ruled by Islam, in which the oppressive Sharia would be the law of the land and all non-Muslims would be subservient or face the sword of Islam. Under such a scenario, the secular Left, with its opposition to most "organized religion", would be victimized no less than their ideological counterparts on the religious Right who proudly identify as Christians or as religious Jews. What possible motivation could these two movements with such sharply contrasting goals have to cooperate with each other?

The answer is actually quite simple. They share two common enemies. The first is often referred to as Judeo-Christian civilization, which is the basis, or at least the root, of Western civilization as we know it today. The prevalent (though evolving) moral concepts that are rooted in the Ten Commandments and the Bible are still the foundations on which that civilization will stand or, if it abandons it, will fall. Many of the pet causes of the far secular Left come into conflict when confronted with the Ten Commandments and the biblical worldview, because that Judeo-Christian worldview denotes a responsibility to the society at large, insisting that without a moral system rooted in the importance of the nuclear family and belief in God, the society will eventually self-destruct in an orgy of hedonism and nihilism.

> *We have no government armed with power capable of contending with human passions unbridled by morality and religion. Avarice, ambition, revenge, or gallantry would break the strongest cords of our Constitution as a whale goes through a net. Our Constitution was made only for a moral and religious people. It is wholly inadequate to the government of any other.*[16]
>
> (John Adams, speech to the US military,
> October 11, 1798)

> *A Bible and a newspaper in every house, a good school in every district – all studied and appreciated as they merit – are the principal support of virtue, morality, and civil liberty.*[17]
>
> (Benjamin Franklin, in a letter
> to the Ministry of France, March 1778)

The secular Left's hatred for America's biblical heritage is almost matched by its aversion towards Israel, which long ago ceased to be one of their favorite causes. Perhaps the animosity comes from Israel's move towards a robust and enterprising capitalist economy in recent years, in abandonment of its socialist founders' ideology. Perhaps it could be due to Israel's increasing insistence on its right to its unique cultural-religious heritage as a Jewish state, which has far more in common with its biblical principles than it does with the Communist Manifesto. Conversely, it could have more to do with left-wing global alliances with the many Third World and Islamic nations who support the destruction of little Israel. In any event, the fact is that Israel's strongest supporters these days are found from the center to the right of the political spectrum, with far too many members of the Left chanting the fictional mantra of the Palestinian people, and perhaps even naively believing in that false narrative more than some of the Muslims do.

It is that dual animosity towards Judeo-Christian civilization and the State of Israel that has animated the alliance of the Islamic ideologues with the secular Left. Furthermore, there is also a commonality of strategy pulling these two groups together. The strategy of deception is firmly rooted in the philosophical heritage of the American Left, as evidenced in the writings of the American Left's intellectual guru from Chicago, Saul Alinsky. Alinsky described himself as a "rebel" and devoted his life to organizing a revolution in America to destroy a system that he regarded as oppressive and unjust. By profession, he was a "community organizer", the same term eventually employed by his most famous disciple, Barack Obama, to describe himself. Though he passed away in 1972, not having met the young Obama personally, the Alinsky model became the Obama strategy, in which he was trained in Chicago and which he also taught in (the large radical social action organization) ACORN's training institute.[18]

Just a few years earlier, in 1969, another young radical student by the name of Hillary Rodham (later Clinton) interviewed Alinsky and wrote her thesis on his theories. In her conclusion, she favorably compared him to Eugene Debs,

Far Left Ideologue: *Apparently a role model for American politicians such as Barack Obama and Hillary Clinton, theoretician Saul Alinsky promoted the strategy of deception to attain the political goals of the radical Left.*

Walt Whitman, and Martin Luther King Jr. The title of her thesis was, "There is Only the Fight: An Analysis of the Alinsky Model". In this title, she singled out what she considered to be Alinsky's most important contribution to the radical cause – his embrace of political nihilism. In other words, the specific cause – even popular leftist causes like abortion rights, gay marriage, or what they self-righteously call social justice – is not the issue. The issue is the accumulation of power to attain the revolution, and any means can be used to achieve the end goal – even outright deception – it is okay and in fact advisable to say anything and pretend to be anything to get what you want. Deception is the radical's most important weapon, and it has been a prominent one since the end of the 1960s. Racial arsonists such as Al Sharpton and Jeremiah Wright have posed as civil rights activists; anti-American radicals such as William Ayers pose as patriotic progressives; socialists pose as liberals. The mark of their success is reflected in the fact that conservatives collude in the deceptions and call them liberals as well.[19]

It's also instructive to point out that on the semantic battleground in the Middle East as well, the Right often succumbs to the power of aggressive left-wing deception, referring to "the Palestinian people", "the West Bank", or the "irreversibility of the peace process", without pointing out the blatant falsehood inherent in the terms and the deception inherent therein. Thus, even far-Left Jewish organizations like J Street pose as "Zionists" who just happen to care about the Palestinian cause, and therefore, are able to call for an independent Palestinian state with Jerusalem as its capital and not be accused of being anti-Israel. This is classic deception, newspeak designed to mislead and pervert, in order to attain the vaunted end goal of destroying Israel's territorial integrity, while masquerading as sincere Zionist Jews who want to save Israel from itself.

> *Conservatives think of war as a metaphor when applied to politics. For radicals, the war is real. That is why when partisans of the Left go into battle, they set out to destroy their opponents by stigmatizing them as "racists," "sexists," "homophobes" and "Islamophobes." It is also why they so often pretend to be what they are not ("liberals" for example) and rarely say what they mean. Deception for them is a military tactic in a war that is designed to eliminate the enemy.[20]*
>
> (Political analyst and former radical leftist David Horowitz)

We see that the accepted political strategy model of the 2012 Democratic Party leadership jibed neatly with the Islamic political strategy model of taqiyya. The ramifications of this are quite disturbing and are in sharp contradiction to the Western concept of truthfulness that is rooted in the Bible of Israel.

> *From a false matter you shall keep far.*
>
> (Exodus 23:7)

> *You shall not steal, neither shall you deal falsely, nor lie one to another.*
>
> (Leviticus 19:11)

> *Deceit is abominable to Him.*
>
> (Proverbs 12:22)

For those cynics who don't care what the Bible says, a few words need to be said here about the Bible, the all-time bestseller, which has been greatly ridiculed in recent years. There are many Americans who regard it, at best, as a work of great literature, but we who live in Israel know that extensive archeological

God And The Bible: *According to America's first President, George Washington, the eternal biblical truths and guidelines were a central component in one's ability to govern a nation.*

finds have verified so many of the biblical descriptions, and therefore, whatever one's religious beliefs may be, the fact is that there is much truth within its covers, both historical and moral. This author will not submit to the anti-biblical arrogance that is indeed an affront, not just to Israel and the Jewish people, but to the roots of Western civilization. Let's take a look at what just some of the American Founding Fathers and Presidents said about this:

It is impossible to rightly govern the world without God and the Bible.[21]

(George Washington)

I have always said and always will say that the studious perusal of the Sacred Volume will make better citizens, better fathers, better husbands ... the Bible makes the best people in the world.[22]

(Thomas Jefferson)

My custom is to read four or five chapters of the Bible every morning immediately after rising ... It seems to me the most suitable manner of beginning the day ... It is an invaluable and inexhaustible mine of knowledge and virtue.[23]

(John Quincy Adams)

But for this book we could not know right from wrong.[24]

(Abraham Lincoln)

The Bible is the Word of Life. I beg that you will read it and find this out for yourselves. Read, not little snatches here and there, but long passages that will really be the road to the heart of it.[25]

(Woodrow Wilson)

The fundamental basis of this nation's law was given to Moses on the Mount ... I don't think we emphasize that enough these days. If we don't have the proper fundamental moral background, we will finally end up with a totalitarian government which does not believe in rights for anybody except the state.[26]

(Harry S. Truman)

Within the covers of the Bible are the answers for all the problems men face.[27]

(Ronald Reagan)

Yes, it has become a common value in America and in much of Western civilization that honesty is paramount, and the legendary story of George Washington and the cherry tree attests to that,[28] but when that value is being challenged by liars, whether secular and Islamic, we need to remember where our values come from, and that source is the original Hebrew Bible.

It's no accident that the chancellor of Harvard University in colonial times was an ardent Hebraist and that Hebrew was a prerequisite in most Ivy League schools.[29] The Christians who established the United States understood that the Bible would be its moral basis, the rock on which it would stand. Since most of the teachings of Jesus also come from the Torah, it is clear that the root of Judeo-Christian civilization is the Bible of Israel.

A Heritage Of Responsibility Based On The Book: *British Prime Minister Margaret Thatcher, often called "The Iron Lady", was known for her firmness in politics and leadership, but the basis of that strength was her firmness of belief in the heritage of Western civilization, which she asserted was derived from the Bible of Israel.*

It isn't merely about democracy and liberty ... It is personal liberty with personal responsibility ... responsibility to your parents, to your children, to your God. This really binds us together in a way that nothing else does. If you accept freedom, you've got to have principles about the responsibility. You can't do this without a biblical foundation.[30]

(Margaret Thatcher)

We have to remember that the Jewish people never, ever lost their faith in the face of all the persecution and as a result have come to have their own promised land and to have Jerusalem as a capital city again.[31]

(Margaret Thatcher)

As with many Americans and others in our current Western civilization, many Israelis don't want to accept that our heritage is rooted in that book, partially because the ramifications of that acceptance wouldn't fit neatly with the belief that peace can be attained through negotiation with our Islamic neighbors. The reality is that there is a clash of civilizations going on, a religious war of values and potential domination by an Islamic culture that has brought backwardness, and savage, abusive behavior and repression to virtually every country that it has conquered. If it wasn't for the vast oil reserves in the Persian Gulf, the entire Muslim world would still be in poverty. Even so, much of it still is.

In a March 2010 discussion between Israeli Knesset Member Tzippi Livni and US Foreign Relations Committee Chairman Senator John Kerry (D-MA), Livni lamented that "the diplomatic conflict between Israel and the Palestinians is about to turn into a religious one that will be impossible to solve."[32]

The problem is that what she called the "diplomatic process" had long ago already become a religious conflict. In fact, it always has been.

In our time, we have witnessed the Arab Spring, the breakdown of negotiations with the PA and the rapidly rising tensions between Israel and Iran, which is intent on destroying the Jewish state, perhaps with a nuclear bomb that it is frantically working to develop. Can we truly understand these tumultuous events as mere diplomacy, or do we need to view them in the often unpleasant context of religious conflict?

CHAPTER SEVEN

The Arab Spring

Democracy is two wolves and a lamb voting on what to have for lunch. Liberty is a well-armed lamb contesting the vote![1]

(Benjamin Franklin)

D ecember of 2010: The excitement in the air was palpable and its shouts echoed around the world at the speed of light on every television, on every computer, and in every home. The Arab world, having long suffered under the yoke of ruthless dictators and not so benevolent kings, was rebelling, calling for freedom and democracy. Anyone watching these rose-colored news reports might have been forgiven for seeing images of Benjamin Franklin, Thomas Jefferson, Abraham Lincoln, and Martin Luther King Jr. hovering over these massive demonstrations in Tahrir Square in Cairo, Egypt.

Hundreds of thousands, even millions of protesters had gathered to demand the resignation of Egyptian President Hosni Mubarak, after thirty years of strong-armed rule. To the Western world, it was known at first as the pro-democracy movement, but soon came to be referred to as the Arab Spring, giving it a very optimistic feeling and a positive spin, but is it really positive? Has it truly been a movement that is expanding freedom in the Middle East, strengthening human rights, and bringing genuine peace between Israel and its neighbors?

Let's begin our analysis by reviewing this encyclopedia

Give Me Islamic Sharia Law Or Give Me Death: *The Tahrir Square demonstrations in Egypt were not a quest for American-style democracy, but rather a demand for elections so that the oppressive Islamic Sharia law could be imposed on the Egyptian population, Muslims and non-Muslims alike.*

overview (very slightly modified for accuracy and clarity) of the Arab Spring:

> *The Arab Spring, also known as the Arab Revolution is a revolutionary wave of demonstrations and protests occurring in the Arab world that began on 18 December 2010.*
>
> *To date, rulers have been forced from power in Tunisia, Egypt, Libya, and Yemen; civil uprisings have erupted in Bahrain and Syria; major protests have broken out in Algeria, Iraq, Jordan, Kuwait, Morocco, and Sudan; and minor protests have occurred in Lebanon, Mauritania, Oman, Saudi Arabia, Jordan, Djibouti, and Western Sahara. Clashes at the borders of Israel in May 2011, and the protests by the Arab minority in Iranian Khuzestan*

erupted in 2011 as well. Weapons and Tuareg fighters returning from the Libyan civil war stoked a simmering rebellion in Mali, and the consequent Malian coup d'état has been described as "fallout" from the Arab Spring in North Africa. The sectarian clashes in Lebanon were described as a spillover violence of the Syrian uprising and hence the regional Arab Spring. Most recently, in September 2012, a wave of social protests swept the Palestinian Authority, demanding lower consumer prices and resignation of the Palestinian Prime Minister Fayyad.

The protests have shared techniques of mostly civil resistance in sustained campaigns involving strikes, demonstrations, marches, and rallies, as well as the effective use of social media to organize, communicate, and raise awareness in the face of state attempts at repression and Internet censorship.

Many Arab Spring demonstrations have met violent responses from authorities, as well as from pro-government militias and counter-demonstrators. These attacks have been answered with violence from protestors in some cases. A major slogan of the demonstrators in the Arab world has been "the people want to bring down the regime".

Some observers have drawn comparisons between the Arab Spring movements and the pro-democratic, anti-Communist Revolutions of 1989 (also known as the Autumn of Nations) that swept through Eastern Europe and the Communist world, in terms of their scale and significance. Others, however, have pointed out that there are several key differences between the movements, such as the desired outcomes and the organizational role of (internet) technology in the Arab revolutions.[2]

So who was right? Was the Arab Spring simply a replay of 1989? Were those in Eastern Europe and the former Soviet Union seeking free elections for the same purposes as the Arab

Spring protesters?

The fall of the Berlin Wall separating then West Germany from Soviet Communist dominated East Germany was an event that was soon followed by the fall of the entire Soviet bloc of Communism, which was replaced by political systems roughly resembling those in the West. It was motivated, in most cases, by a true thirsting for American-style liberty and religious expression. The free countries that emerged soon aligned themselves with the United States and Western Europe. In contrast to this, and despite its inspirational name, the Arab Spring is an altogether different movement, with an altogether different agenda.

Arab spokesmen often are sharply critical of those in the West who criticize the Arab Spring for failing to live up to the standards of American-style freedom. They refer to American arrogance, charging that it's unfair for Americans, as well as some Europeans, to judge the Arab world based on Western norms and Western values. A case in point was Presidential candidate Mitt Romney's comment, on a 2012 visit to Israel, about sharp differences in achievement between the Palestinian Authority and Israel, despite massive financial support for the PA from nations around the world.

> *Culture makes all the difference. And as I come here and I look out over this city and consider the accomplishments of the people of this nation, I recognize the power of at least culture and a few other things.*[3]
>
> (Mitt Romney, speaking in Jerusalem, 2012)

The Arab world appeals to the vaunted American tolerance, demanding respect for their Middle Eastern way of life and asking for patience and continued support as the new regimes develop their constitutions and their governmental systems. To some extent, they are correct. No one can claim that the Arab Spring is not an indigenous, popular movement with unique Arab or Islamic characteristics, which define the direction and flavor of its development. As we discussed earlier, it is a natural outgrowth of a different culture which is in conflict with Judeo-Christian civilization, because it is neither Judaic nor is it Christian. In fact, it is a rejection of both and the ultimate goal is to dominate, not just the Middle East, but the entirety of Judeo-Christian civilization.

> *Islam isn't in America to be equal to any other faith, but to become dominant. The Koran ... should be the highest authority in America, and Islam the only accepted religion on earth.*[4]

(Omar M. Ahmad,
Chairman of CAIR,
the Council for American Islamic Relations)

Most of the reports about the Arab Spring fell short in their accuracy for several reasons, but the primary shortcoming was the failure to identify the major catalysts behind the Arab Spring. No, it was not the seemingly secular college students who provided the impetus and momentum for the movement, although they were the most visible in the Western media, thus providing an acceptable Westernized face to the folks in America and Europe. It took days and even a few weeks until it gradually became clear that the rebellion had been fomented by none other than the radical Muslim Brotherhood, the long repressed but potent political/religious organization that seeks Islamic dominance around the world. Upon hearing and viewing the initial news reports about the wonderful "pro-democracy" movement in Egypt, I was immediately skeptical. In the broader view of history, culture, and religion, it didn't make sense. There was something incongruent here that told me that we had been in this movie before some twenty-five years earlier.

Flashback 1978: Huge demonstrations in the streets of Tehran, Iran as the masses call for an end to the decades long rule of Mohammad Reza Pahlavi, known to all as the Shah of Iran. The demonstrations appear to have arisen as a spontaneous outburst of a longing for freedom, directed against the Shah, the autocratic ruler who had, against the wishes of the more dogmatic Islamic ideologues, increasingly modernized and westernized his country during his 30-plus years of power. So, too, much of the opposition derived from his iron-fisted grip on what many considered to be his increasingly imperial power. Despite a parliamentary system, he was the clear and undisputed monarch and he steered his nation in a direction that he saw as beneficial to Iran's growth and development. As the years passed, he built a strongly cooperative relationship with the United States on many levels. The Shah had even developed a secretly cooperative economic and military relationship with Israel. While very cautious, because of the Islamic taboo, not to speak positively about Israel in public, the Shah nevertheless rightly recognized Israel as the only other pro-Western nation in the Middle East and an American ally that he could work with. Furthermore, he understood the benefit of covert strategic cooperation with a Jewish state that had a burgeoning military industry. Israel viewed Iran as part of its strategy to develop ties with non-Arab states on the region's periphery, such as Turkey and Ethiopia. It also saw Iran as an important way station for Jews fleeing persecution in Iraq. Furthermore, the two nations had a mutual economic relationship in trade, including the sale of Iranian oil to Israel.

"Under the Shah, Israeli-Iranian ties were multi-layered and complex," said Haim Malka, a Middle East expert at the Center for Strategic and International Studies in Washington. "The Shah had a similar interest in building strategic ties with Israel, a growing military power that had a record of defeating Arab armies, though he was careful not to publicly embrace Israel too warmly," Malka said. It was "a love affair without marriage," said David Menashri, an Israeli expert on Israeli-Iranian relations, quoting an Iranian diplomat. "You don't need to have a formal contract to have a happy marriage. You are happy together."[5] Even though Iran never formally recognized Israel, the Jewish state operated a permanent delegation in Iran until the overthrow of the Shah in 1979.

The outer face of (what was reported in the media as) the Iranian pro-democracy movement appeared to be an alliance between Islamic groups and an array of opposition groups including constitutionalist liberals – the democratic, reformist Islamic Freedom Movement of Iran, headed by Mehdi Bazargan, and the more secular National Front. They were based in the urban middle class, and wanted the Shah to adhere to the Iranian Constitution of 1906 rather than to replace him with a theocracy.

Stood In The Way Of The Islamic Revolution: *The Shah of Iran was an ally of the United States and a secret ally of Israel, until he was overrun by his country's Islamic fundamentalists.*

Demonstrations against the Shah commenced in October 1977, developing into a widespread campaign of civil resistance that was partly secular and partly religious, and intensifying in January 1978. Between August and December 1978, strikes and demonstrations paralyzed the country. Nonetheless, it soon became apparent that the driving force, indeed the more numerous, better organized, and cohesive catalyst behind the revolution was the Shiite Muslim movement of Ayatollah Ruhollah Khomeini. Eventually, succumbing to the pressure of the revolution while simultaneously battling an advanced stage of cancer, the Shah left Iran for exile on January 16, 1979 as the last Persian monarch. In the resulting power vacuum

The Muslim Brotherhood Of Its Time: *More numerous, better organized, and more cohesive than the secular Left, the catalyst behind the Islamic revolution in Iran was the Shiite Muslim movement of Ayatollah Ruhollah Khomeini.*

that was created by the Shah's departure, Ayatollah Khomeini returned to Tehran two weeks later to a rousing welcome by several million Iranians. The royal reign collapsed shortly after on February 11, when guerrillas and rebel troops overwhelmed troops loyal to the Shah in armed street fighting. Iran voted by national referendum to become an Islamic Republic on April 1, 1979, and to approve a new democratic-theocratic hybrid constitution whereby Khomeini became Supreme Leader of the country, in December 1979.[6] The rise to power of the Islamic ideologues in Iran almost immediately led to a flexing of muscles and a crisis with the United States, during which 52 Americans were held hostage for 444 days from November 4, 1979, to January 20, 1981, after a group of Islamic students and militants took over the American Embassy in Tehran in a show of support for the Iranian Revolution and anger towards "the Great Satan" ("The Little Satan" in their semantics being Israel).[7] The Islamic theocracy has been in power in Iran ever since and has, undisputedly, been the most consistent supporter of Islamic terrorism in the Middle East and throughout the world. Furthermore, it has been quite transparent about its intention to export that revolution to the free world.

> *We shall export our revolution to the whole world. Until the cry ... There is no god but Allah ... resounds over the whole world, there will be struggle.[8]*
> (Ayatollah Ruhollah Khomeini, 1979)

This entire process was viewed helplessly from abroad by American President Jimmy Carter, whose confusing approach to the Shah's rule probably hastened his downfall. When the Shah visited the White House in November 1977, he was the recipient of public expressions of support from the president, but he was later chastised in private meetings by Carter for his spotty human rights record. The Shah was strongly urged to consider reaching out to dissident groups and "easing off" on police actions against them.[9] This pressure was something new to the Shah and the timing of Carter's reprimand couldn't have been worse for the

Fall Of Mubarak, Rise Of Islamic Fundamentalism: *Hosni Mubarak, while a dictator like most in the Islamic world, had maintained a strong relationship with the West and a cold peace with Israel, while preventing the Muslim fundamentalists from contending for power.*

embattled Persian leader, who was already in a fight for both personal and political survival.

Yes, we have been in this movie before. When the revolution began in December of 2010 in the streets of Egypt, the analogy to Iran couldn't have been greater. The Islamic ideologues of Egypt were playing the role of the Iranian Ayatollahs, while Egyptian President Hosni Mubarak was the Shah of Iran and President Barack Obama was Jimmy Carter. Likewise, both rebel movements had been portrayed as primarily secular, freedom-loving movements until it became clear that the Islamic genie was hiding in the wings. In both cases, it soon emerged in all of its passion and took complete control of both their respective revolutions and their respective nations.

As the Egyptian revolution crystallized, eventually spreading to other countries in the Middle East, it became obvious to all that the Muslim Brotherhood, joined by other even more radical Islamic groups such as the Salafists, was the dominant and most cohesive force in the overthrow of Hosni Mubarak, just as the Ayatollahs were the dominant force in the overthrow of the Shah of Iran. Once it become apparent even to the often fawning members of the media, everyone began scrambling to answer the question that suddenly was on everyone's mind – What is the Muslim Brotherhood and why do we need to be concerned about them?

It's hard to at this point to point to a specific agenda of the Muslim Brotherhood as a group.[10]
(US National Intelligence Director James Clapper, February 2011)

*There are **strains** of their (the Muslim Brotherhood's) ideology that are anti-US.[11]*
(US President Barack Hussein Obama, February 2011)

The ironic thing about this sudden concern was that the Muslim Brotherhood has been around since 1928 and the information has always been out there for those who have cared to read it. Founded in Egypt in 1928, by Hassan al-Banna, a teacher and imam, the goal of the Muslim Brotherhood is global Islamic domination and the establishment of Islamic Sharia law.

The basic doctrine of the group's creed is as follows:

Allah is our objective, the prophet is our leader, the Koran is our law, Jihad is our way, dying in the way of Allah is our highest hope.[12]

Until the revolution in Egypt, very few people in the free world had ever heard of the Muslim Brotherhood, and yet it is considered to be the most influential Islamic movement in the United States and the world. Experts say that every prominent Islamic organization in the US is controlled by the Muslim Brotherhood and some have even called it an "insurgency." It was even reported in Rose El-Youssef, an Egyptian magazine, in December 2012, that six Muslim Brotherhood operatives have infiltrated the Obama administration as senior advisors, including the Department of Homeland Security.

With affiliates and branches in more than 100 countries worldwide, it has inspired radical Islamic movements around the world.

The group had underground links to the Nazis starting in the 1930s and supported terrorism orchestrated by Haj Amin al-Husseini in British Mandatory Palestine.

The late PLO Chairman Yasser Arafat fought alongside the Muslim Brotherhood in the 1940s in his native Egypt, long before he considered himself to be a Palestinian. Al-Qaeda was inspired by the Muslim Brotherhood and Hamas has always considered itself to be "a division of the Muslim Brotherhood in Palestine."[13]

As for Obama's statement that there are only some "strains" of anti-Americanism, let's examine what has been written in their own words:

> *In May 1991, the Muslim Brotherhood issued to its ideological allies an explanatory memorandum on "the General Strategic Goal for the Group in North America." Explaining that the Brotherhood's mission was to establish "an effective and ... stable Islamic Movement" on the continent, this document outlined a "Civilization-Jihadist Process" for achieving that objective. It stated that Muslims "must understand that their work in America is a kind of grand Jihad in eliminating and destroying the Western civilization from within and 'sabotaging' its miserable house by their hands ... so that ... God's religion (Islam) is made victorious over all other religions."[14]*

Are Americans, Canadians, Europeans, and others in the West so near-sighted that they don't see what is staring them in the face? The Arab Spring is not and has never been a friend of the United States or any other Western countries.

A 2010 poll was taken in several Islamic countries by the Pew Education Research Center in which it was found that while most people in countries like Egypt, Jordan, and Pakistan stated a preference for democracy, they also supported laws that don't jibe well with humane laws in the free world today. For example 77% of Egyptians support cutting off the hands of an individual found guilty of theft, while a whopping 84% would support the death penalty for a Muslim who changes his religion.[15] Obviously, we are speaking not about American-style liberty, in which freedom of speech, freedom of the press, and freedom of religion go hand in hand with an extraordinary tolerance towards those who have different opinions. No, we are speaking only about free elections desired for the purpose of creating an intolerant Islamic society.

Free elections, when carried out without having the prerequisite freedoms described above ingrained into the national culture, are a recipe for disaster. Nonetheless, the Obama administration continued to speak of the uprising in Egypt and the process leading to elections and Jihadist victory in Egypt as an example for the world.

> *The Egyptian people have inspired us as they have changed the world.[16]*
>
> (Barack Obama, February 2011)

> *The only foundation of a free Constitution is pure Virtue, and if this cannot be inspired into our People, in a greater Measure than they have it now, they may change their Rulers, and the forms of Government, but they will not obtain a lasting Liberty.[17]*
>
> (John Adams, June 1776)

The Muslim Brotherhood scored a rousing victory in the Egyptian elections, winning the Presidency through their candidate Muhammad Morsi, as well as, together with their (even more extreme) Salafist Muslim allies, a clear majority of the Egyptian Parliament. The results were predictable and they are leading Egypt on the road to Sharia law, support for Islamic terrorist groups and a gradual abrogation of the peace treaty with Israel. It has been followed by a rise in terrorist attacks from the Egyptian-controlled Sinai desert and greater Egyptian involvement in supporting the Hamas terrorist group against Israel.

The Sinai attacks were followed several months later by an attack on the US Embassy in Egypt, in which hundreds of people breached the walls of the US Embassy in Cairo shortly before 9/11 of that year. The protesters tore down an American flag and replaced it with a black Islamic banner adorned with white characters that read, "There is no God but Allah and Mohammed is his messenger."[18]

In neighboring Libya, the process has been similar. The civil war in Libya, also referred to as the Libyan revolution, erupted following protests in Benghazi beginning on February 15, 2011, which led to clashes with security forces. The protests escalated into a rebellion, eventually expanding into a wide-scale conflict between forces loyal to Colonel Muammar Gaddafi and those seeking to oust his government. The war soon spread across the country, with the forces opposing Gaddafi establishing an interim governing body, the National Transitional Council.

After Gaddafi's military cracked down harshly on the rebel militias, the Obama administration and the European Union quickly took sides in the conflict. On March 19, 2011, the United States spearheaded a multi-national coalition led by NATO forces to provide extensive military support to the rebels in their fight against the Libyan government forces. A United Nations resolution authorized member states to establish and enforce a no-fly zone over Libya, and to use "all necessary measures" to prevent attacks on civilians, meaning to prevent attacks on the rebels. Throughout the conflict, the rebels rejected Libyan government offers of a ceasefire and efforts by the African Union to end the fighting because the proposed plans did not include the removal of Gaddafi.

On September 16, 2011, the National Transitional Council was recognized by the United Nations as the legal representative of Libya, replacing the Gaddafi government. Muammar Gaddafi was captured and killed on October 20, 2011, while attempting to escape from rebel pursuit. The National Transitional Council "declared the liberation of Libya" and the official end of the war three days later.[19]

> *The Libyan revolution was the work of ordinary, brave*
> *Libyans who demanded their freedoms and dignity. The*
> *United States is proud to have supported them in those*
> *efforts and we are committed to their future.*[20]
>
> (US Secretary of State Hillary Rodham Clinton,
> October 23, 2011)

Once again, we heard glowing words to describe another milestone of the Arab Spring, but should we have been excited? As with the overthrow of Mubarak in Egypt, the West overthrew a relatively stable regime that had, in recent years, despite its previously erratic leader, found a way to coexist with the free world. Was it worth the billions of dollars spent by NATO in support of the rebels?

The true face of the Libyan revolution soon became apparent in a series of seemingly unrelated events. Let's examine three of them:

1. Shortly after the rebel victory, at a rally in Benghazi, National Transitional Council leader Mustafa Abdul Jalil said, "As a Muslim country, we have adopted the Islamic Sharia as the main source of law. Accordingly, any law that contradicts Islamic principles with the Islamic Sharia is ineffective legally."[21] Hence, there would be no protection of women from wife-beating (permitted under Sharia), no public observance of any religion other than Islam, and no building or repair of non-Muslim places of worship that have fallen into disrepair, but there would be child marriages and polygamy (permitted under Sharia). One has to wonder what values the free world nations thought they were supporting with the NATO attacks.

2. David Gerbi, a Libyan-born Jewish psychoanalyst, lived in exile in Italy for over 40 years. He returned to Libya

with great optimism to assist the Libyan rebel forces during the uprising against Muammar Gaddafi. Gerbi, then 56, provided psychological treatment to Libyan rebel forces during the anti-Gaddafi uprising, and was dubbed the "revolutionary Jew." He had fled Libya with his family when he was 12, but his dream was to return and to rebuild the ancient synagogue in Tripoli and he claimed to have received permission from Libya's interim authorities, the National Transition Council, and a local Muslim cleric to proceed. However, it was not to be. When he entered the synagogue to begin the long process of renovation, wild mobs gathered outside the synagogue threatening to kill him if he continued to carry out his goal of asserting freedom of worship. "They told me that if I am not leaving now, they are going to come and they are going to kill me because they don't want Jews here," a frustrated Gerbi complained, as his security guard whisked him away.[22] Apparently, this well-intentioned Jewish refugee wasn't familiar with the extent of the intolerance in the culture of Sharia law.

3. On September 11, 2012, Islamic terrorists launched an attack on the American consulate in Benghazi, Libya, murdering the US Ambassador Christopher Stevens, as well as three other American officials. The deaths of Ambassador Stevens and the other embassy employees came after a wild mob originally referred to in the media as "protestors", surrounded the Benghazi consulate, ostensibly to protest an internet film critical of Islam's founder Muhammad that had been produced by an Egyptian Christian based in the United States. In Washington, President Barack Hussein Obama strangely accepted this narrative and decried "a senseless act of violence". The mob was armed with guns and rocket-propelled grenades, according to

Terrorists Storm The American Embassy: *Initially reported to be merely a protest against an amateurish movie that was critical of Islam, it soon became clear that this was a full-fledged terrorist attack on the American Embassy in Benghazi, Libya on September 11, 2012.*

The Associated Press,[23] but Secretary of State Hillary Clinton, apparently seeking to deflect criticism of an American policy that downplayed Islamic terrorism as a global threat, emphasized and denounced the little-known video and added as a side note that "violence is unacceptable".[24] UN Ambassador Susan Rice, one of Obama's top advisors, repeatedly referred to the attack as "spontaneous and not premeditated or preplanned."[25] Did she really believe that guns and rocket-propelled grenades are used by spontaneous protestors who are upset about a low-budget film? If it really was spontaneous, then why did it occur on 9/11? Could it possibly be that Islamic terrorist organizations were involved in orchestrating the entire episode?

The rotten fruits of the Arab Spring have been seen throughout the Middle East. The so-called thirsting for freedom of Muslims has been proven to be nothing more than a thirst for Sharia law and the continuation of the Islamic revolution, so it is absolutely absurd and nationally suicidal for the leadership of the free world to show support for such a process. Do Americans, Europeans, and others truly want taxpayer funds to go towards a process that will lead to the banning of all religions other than Islam? Do they really want to encourage a process leading to wife-beating, child marriages, and sexual abuse of children? Could it be that the proponents of freedom actually want to invest in Jihad?

Returning to our central question of peace, we need to ask what the Arab Spring has meant and will mean for the prospect of peace between Israel and its neighbors. If we examine each country in the Middle East with respect to the effects of the Arab Spring and the chance of achieving peace with Israel, we see one clear pattern – peace in the Middle East is certainly not dependent on Israel. Most of the conflicts since the rise of the Arab Spring in December of 2010 have been due to internal Islamic rivalries between Sunni Muslims and Shiite Muslims, while others have arisen from the ascendance of the Muslim Brotherhood and al-Qaeda. Let's examine the major causes and the nature of conflict within each nation or arising from each nation:

Egypt – The so-called pro-democracy rebel movement, which among the Muslim population was primarily but not entirely an Islamic fundamentalist movement was successful due to the assertion of power by the well-organized and popular Muslim Brotherhood and other Islamic fundamentalists. They had previously been banned in Egypt during the Mubarak years following the Brotherhood's assassination of previous President Anwar Sadat. During Mubarak's thirty-year reign, the basic rights of the approximately 10% Christian minority were quietly protected. However, in post-revolution Egypt, the dominancy of Sharia in the proposed constitution has made it clear that the pro-democracy "protesters" were simply exploiting free elections to impose Sharia, which of course is the opposite of a free society. Just ask the beleaguered Christian population in Egypt, suffering under Sharia-based oppression.[26]

President Mohammed Morsi of the Muslim Brotherhood, in classic Islamic deception style, is shielding his views from the international public. All that one needs to do to ascertain his real views is to hear the views that he expressed just two years prior to his election:

> *No reasonable person can expect any progress on this track. Either (you accept) the Zionists and everything they want, or else it is war. This is what these occupiers of the land of Palestine know – these blood-suckers, who attack the Palestinians, these warmongers, the descendants of apes and pigs.[27]*

(Mohammed Morsi, March 2010)

Libya – The rebel movement that militarily overthrew Muammar Gaddafi in Libya was aided greatly by the logistical and outright military support provided by NATO forces, mainly funded by the United States.[28] The pretext for that support was that Libyan dictator Gaddafi was indiscriminately killing Libyan civilians.[29] In reality, he was trying to repress the rebellion. As in the Iranian revolution and the Egyptian revolution, it

Not Just A Buffoon In Costume: *While certainly no past friend of Israel, nor of the West, Muammar Gaddafi had established some stability in Libya's foreign relationships several years before his downfall by agreeing to end his WMD (weapons of mass destruction) program.*

soon became clear that Muslim fundamentalists were the most cohesive faction in the rebel alliance, with Muslim Brotherhood (banned under Gaddafi since 1949), al-Qaeda, and other fundamentalist activists greatly influencing the march towards anti-American activity. If there was any doubt, it was pushed aside when the leader of the Libyan Transitional Government, considered to be relatively pro-Western, made it clear that Sharia law would be the basis of Libyan jurisprudence. While the fundamentalists as a party may not yet be in total control of the Libyan government, their influence remains strong and their push for Sharia will continue.

Syria – Syrian dictator Bashar Assad, succeeding his father, Hafez Assad, had ruled with an iron fist since being handed power after his father's death in June of 2000. As in Egypt and Libya, while it can be argued that the Syrian rebels are seeking democratic elections, they certainly are not seeking what those in the West consider to be democratic freedoms, such as freedom of religion, freedom of speech, and freedom of the press. Here, too, the Muslim Brotherhood (banned in Syria under the Assads since 1980) is dominant in the rebel organizers and forces. It has been reported that al-Qaeda is very active as well in the Syrian anti-Assad forces.[30] What distinguishes Syria from Egypt and Libya, making the animosity more intense and particularly violent, is the ethnic, internal Islamic rivalry in this conflict. Assad is an Alawite, an offshoot of Shiite Islam and he is closely aligned with both Iran and the Hezbollah terrorist organization in Lebanon, while his opponents are Sunnis. Therefore, the resultant civil war should have come as no surprise, with Iran and Hezbollah providing support to Assad, while Sunni-dominated countries like Saudi Arabia, Turkey, and Qatar are backing the Sunni Muslim Brotherhood-led rebels. If the rebels are victorious, it seems likely that they will follow the Muslim Brotherhood path to Sharia and hostility towards the West and Israel.

The Shiite-Sunni animosity is further seen in the oil-rich Persian Gulf countries, where Shiite rebels supported by Iran have been agitating for the overthrow of the Sunni-dominated monarchies. In a revealing statement at the conclusion of a two-day summit in December 2012, the (Sunni-dominated) Gulf Cooperation Council members voiced support for Bahrain's Sunni minority regime while lashing out at Shiite-ruled Iran, which they accused of fueling a Shiite-led uprising in the Bahrain last year. The six Sunni-Muslim-ruled states – Saudi Arabia, Qatar, Bahrain, Kuwait, Oman, and the United Arab Emirates – also condemned Iran's "continued occupation of the three Emirati islands" of Abu Musa, Greater Tunb and Lesser Tunb, which lie in the strategic Strait of Hormuz entrance to the Gulf. The regional powers have also taken opposite stances towards the Syrian crisis. While Tehran has openly supported President Bashar al-Assad's regime, GCC members Saudi Arabia and Qatar have blatantly been arming Sunni-Muslim rebels fighting Alawite/Shiite-allied Assad regime loyalists.[31]

From its onset, President Barack Obama was full of praise for the Arab Spring as a great movement, and provided substantial American financial and military support to its victors. However, the prevalent view that financial aid will buy friendship and adherence to American values is naive at best. The Arab Spring has seriously destabilized the entire region and has greatly strengthened the most ideological forces in Sunni Islam, who now have joined their Shiite counterparts in their fierce opposition to Judeo-Christian values and their uncompromising hostility to Israel. Since the Muslim Brotherhood's triumph in Egypt, President Muhammad Morsi has been quietly informing his people about the eventual abrogation of the Sadat-Begin peace treaty with Israel, while simultaneously sending comforting words to the Americans about his desire to adhere to all international treaties. Thus, he is able to calm his hard-core Islamic supporters who are agitating for the break-off of ties with Israel, while at the same time insuring the continued flow of money from the American administration.

Jews have increased the corruption in the world, and

... shed the blood of Muslims ... Muslims must realize that restoring the sanctuaries and protecting honor and blood from the hands of Jews will not happen through the parlors of the United Nations, or through negotiations. The Zionists only know the way of force.[32]

(Mohammed Badie, spiritual guide of
Egypt's Muslim Brotherhood, October 2012)

Heavily-armed Egypt, to the south of Israel, has become a potentially hostile and dangerous enemy, with 77% of Egyptians in an October 2012 poll calling for the abrogation of the peace treaty with Israel and 87% wanting Egypt to have its own nuclear bomb.[33]

Israel is now surrounded on all sides by forces seeking its destruction. Directly north of Israel is Lebanon, where the Hezbollah terrorist organization has seized control, both militarily and electorally, and has established a potent base from which to strike Israel with its enormous stockpile of Iranian-supplied missiles. To the northeast is Syria, with a supply of weapons of mass destruction (WMD) unrivaled among Israel's neighbors. The Syrian WMD reportedly include substantial amounts of chemical and biological weapons. Given the ongoing Syrian civil war, it's anyone's guess in whose hands they will end up, but one thing is clear – barring an Israeli preemptive strike – there is no doubt that they will end up in the hands of Israel's enemies. To the South, of course is Muslim Brotherhood-dominated Egypt and Hamas-dominated Gaza. Last but not least, on the eastern side of Israel, and sharing the longest border, is the Kingdom of Jordan, officially in a peace treaty with Israel, where King Abdullah is trying appease an increasingly emboldened Muslim Brotherhood by throwing it economic bones, political bones, and verbal bones in the form of public criticism of Israel. He has to date managed to repress the opposition, but the demands for political reforms are growing and as this process continues, it will be led by the Brotherhood, either openly or covertly. The next step is known to all, as the Arab Spring continues.

Chapter Eight

Israel-Arab Peace:
Facing The Main Issues

Given the difficult regional and cultural/religious challenges, is peace between Israel and its neighbors truly a realistic possibility? If not, what is?

In order to answer that question, we need first to seriously examine the true meaning of certain central issues: settlement, refugees, and land for peace. These issues go to the core of the inability to achieve peace despite all of the political, financial, and other efforts expended and invested in the process. The peace process has become the holy cow of the Middle East, the seemingly sacred process that supposedly needs to be taking place at all times. An American president, as well as an Israeli prime minister, is not considered to be responsible if he is not taking action in pushing forward the peace process. However, the basic premise is flawed. The belief that we always need to be creating and pursuing comprehensive peace plans for their own sake and engaging in peace negotiations and bombastic summits is in fact based on false pretenses. Let's examine these central issues one by one:

Settlement – The Arab Muslim narrative has always referred to the settlements as an obstacle to peace, always focusing on the Jewish communities in Judea and Samaria (the West Bank), but usually including eastern Jerusalem, as well. This is when they are speaking a language other than Arabic. When they speak to their own people in their own language, they invariably refer to the entire land of Israel as settlements. To them, Tel Aviv is a settlement as well. Without truly understanding the meaning of the term settlement in Israel today, one cannot judge the conflict fairly. In the land of Israel, settlement can more accurately be called resettlement, as most of the communities in Israel today (of course including those in post-1967 Israel as well) are reestablished communities that had already existed and thrived in biblical times. In those times, the term settlement would have been most appropriate because it was then that Jewish communities had been established in the land of Israel for the first time, subsequently growing into populous cities and towns. The process of growth continued for well over a thousand years of Jewish residency as the dominant population in Israel.

Those Demonized West Bank Settlements: *After the Six Day War in 1967, when Israel recaptured its biblical heartland, it began to allow Jewish families to return to the communities that had been the heart of their people for well over 3,000 years. Here we see some of the children at play in their community school.*

In 1200 BCE (Before the Common Era, or BC), during the biblical period of the Judges, the Jews were already sovereign in the land of Israel. In 1000 BCE, King David established the unified Kingdom of Israel, with Jerusalem as its capital. There were approximately two million Jews living in Judea and Samaria (the area that in modern times became known as the "West Bank" of the Jordan River) with King David as overall leader. This area was at the center of King David's Kingdom.

In 965 BCE, King Solomon began to build the first Temple on the Temple Mount in Jerusalem which became the focal point of Jewish life forever and until today.

In 586 BCE, the Babylonians destroyed the first Temple and the whole of Jerusalem, after defeating Israel. Most of the Jews were exiled to Babylon. Up to this point in time, the Jews had inhabited, ruled and owned the Land of Israel, including Judea and Samaria, for over 600 years.

In 538 BCE the Jews were allowed to return to Jerusalem to rebuild the Temple and this process began in 516 BCE.

Until 63 CE (the Common Era, or AD), the area was controlled by the Greeks and the Romans but all the Jews were allowed to remain, so for nearly 450 years, in addition to the above 600 years, Judea and Samaria was inhabited by the Jewish people, whose population increased dramatically.

In 63 CE, Pompey, the Roman military leader, conquered Judea and Samaria including Jerusalem and brought this area under total Roman control. (The Roman rule lasted for 7 centuries until the Arab conquest which took place between 634 CE and 642 CE.)

In 70 CE, the Romans under Titus defeated the Jews living in Jerusalem, destroyed the city, occupied Jerusalem and destroyed the second Temple.[1]

The exiled Jews were scattered around the world, but there always remained small pockets of Jews living in the land of Israel, which the Roman conquerors had renamed Palestina, a name that stuck, eventually evolving into Palestine. Some 1,800 years later, the Jews started to return, building various kinds of agricultural settlements and small municipal settlements. All new communities, as well as renewed communities within Israel's capital city Jerusalem were referred to as settlements (yishuvim-plural, or yishuv-singular, in Hebrew). Even Tel Aviv was referred to as a yishuv, because it was a renewed community, built as an extension of the older city of Jaffa.

After the Six Day War in 1967, when Israel recaptured its biblical heartland, regions of Samaria (north of Jerusalem), Judea (south of Jerusalem), and the Old City of Jerusalem itself, the process of Jews returning to reestablish the ancient cities began. The new communities, many of which were built in the same locations as the old ones, were known as new settlements, but the term had positive, idealistic connotations, because in the Israeli culture, resettling and restoring the land to what was is a central Zionist value, actively furthering the return to Jewish sovereignty in the land of Israel. Communities were being established on land that was the heritage of the Israeli nation for well over 3000 years and had now fallen back into its hands in a defensive war. It should be remembered that this was land that was not previously part of any sovereign, independent state of any nation other than Israel, so the Geneva Conventions do not apply there. For those who are unfamiliar with that particular diplomatic dagger that is frequently used to stab Israel with, let's read what it actually says, but first we need to understand the background:

Immediately after the Second World War, the need arose to draft an international convention to protect civilians in times of armed conflict in light of the massive numbers of civilians forced to leave their homes during the war, and the glaring lack of effective protection for civilians under any of the then valid conventions or treaties. In this context, the sixth paragraph of Article 49 of the Fourth Geneva Convention states:

> *The Occupying Power shall not deport or transfer parts of its own civilian population into the territory it occupies.*[2]

The international lawyer Prof. Eugene V. Rostow, a former dean of Yale Law School and Undersecretary of State, stated in 1990:

The Convention prohibits many of the inhumane practices of the Nazis and the Soviet Union during and before the Second World War – the mass transfer of people into and out of occupied territories for purposes of extermination, slave labor or colonization, for example ... The Jewish settlers in the West Bank are most emphatically volunteers. They have not been "deported" or "transferred" to the area by the Government of Israel, and their movement involves none of the atrocious purposes or harmful effects on the existing population it is the goal of the Geneva Convention to prevent.[3]

The 2012 Levy Report, officially known as the "Report on the Legal Status of Building in Judea and Samaria" is an 89-page report on the settlements in Judea and Samaria. It was published on July 9, 2012 after extensive legal and historical research by a three-member committee headed by former Israeli Supreme Court justice Edmund Levy.[4]

The report states as follows:

No analogy should be drawn between Article 49 of the Fourth Geneva Convention and Jewish settlement in Judea and Samaria, in light of the status of the territory under international law, and for that matter a brief history is required.

On 2 November 1917, Lord James Balfour, the British foreign minister, issued a declaration that *"His Majesty's Government view with favour the establishment in Palestine of a national home for the Jewish people"*, the document which was addressed to Lord Rothschild read:

His Majesty's Government view with favour the establishment in Palestine of a national home for the

The Jewish Homeland: *Lord James Balfour, the British foreign minister, best known in Israel for his Balfour Declaration of 1917, called for a Jewish national home in the territory of the British Mandate, which then included both banks of the Jordan River.*

Jewish people, and will use their best endeavours to facilitate the achievement of this object, it being clearly understood that nothing shall be done which may prejudice the civil and religious rights of existing non-Jewish communities in Palestine, or the rights and political status enjoyed by Jews in any other country.

In this declaration Britain recognized the Jewish people's right to the Land of Israel, and even expressed its willingness to advance a process that would eventually lead to the establishment of a national home for them in this part of the world.

This declaration appeared, in a different version, in the declaration of the San Remo Peace Conference in Italy which laid the grounds for the Mandate for Palestine which acknowledged the Jewish people's historic connection to Palestine:

The Mandatory will be responsible for putting into effect the declaration originally made on November 2, 1917, by the British Government, and adopted by the other Allied Powers, in favour of the establishment in Palestine of a national home for the Jewish people, it being clearly understood that nothing shall be done which may prejudice the civil and religious rights of existing non-Jewish communities in Palestine, or the rights and political status enjoyed by Jews in any other country ...

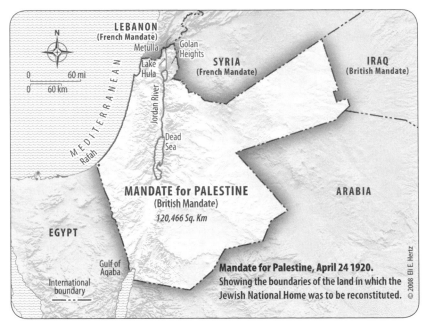

MANDATE for PALESTINE (British Mandate) 120,466 Sq. Km

Mandate for Palestine, April 24 1920. Showing the boundaries of the land in which the Jewish National Home was to be reconstituted.

A Territory Resembling The Size Of Biblical Israel: *The British Mandate, which was authorized by the League of Nations, extended from the Mediterranean Sea all the way to Iraq.*

Recognition had thereby been given to the historical connection of the Jewish people with Palestine and to the grounds for reconstituting their national home in that country.

It should be emphasized here that in the Mandate (as well as in the Balfour Declaration) only the "civil and religious" rights of the inhabitants of Palestine are mentioned as rendering protection, but there is no mention of the national rights of the Arab people. And concerning the actual implementation of this declaration, Article 2 of the Mandate says:

> *The Mandatory shall be responsible for placing the country under such political, administrative and economic conditions as will secure the establishment of the Jewish national home, as laid down in the preamble, and the development of self-governing institutions, and also for safeguarding the civil and religious rights of*

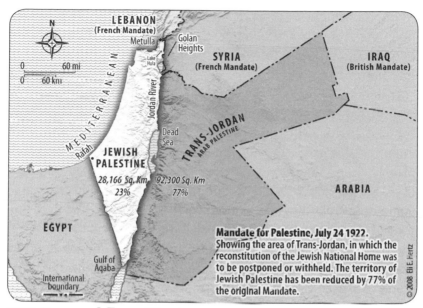

Mandate for Palestine, July 24 1922. Showing the area of Trans-Jordan, in which the reconstitution of the Jewish National Home was to be postponed or withheld. The territory of Jewish Palestine has been reduced by 77% of the original Mandate.

77% Removed From The Embryonic Jewish State *In 1922, the British cut off 77% of the land of their mandate from their previously declared intention to establish a Jewish national home and turned it over to the Hashemite family from the Arabian Peninsula for a new country, to be called Transjordan, meaning "across the Jordan River". The remaining 23%, while greatly reduced, still included Judea, Samaria, the Golan Heights, and all of Jerusalem.*

all the inhabitants of Palestine, irrespective of race and religion.

And in article 6 of the Mandate it says:

The Administration of Palestine, while ensuring that the rights and position of other sections of the population are not prejudiced, shall facilitate Jewish immigration under suitable conditions and shall encourage, in cooperation with the Jewish agency, referred to in Article 4, close settlement by Jews, on the land, including State lands and waste lands not required for public purposes.

In August 1922, the League of Nations approved the

Mandate which was given to Britain, and thus the Jewish people's right to settle in the Land of Israel, their historic homeland, and to establish their state there, was recognized in international law.[5]

Therefore, even if we intentionally put aside what might be referred to as the "religious arguments", meaning legitimate biblical, historical claims buttressing Israel's right to establish communities in Judea and Samaria, the modern legal research clearly shows that Israel has the right to allow Jews to move to these regions and to build communities there. Recent revisionist spin notwithstanding, the international legal basis, sanction, and indeed, encouragement for Jewish settlement was there – from the Balfour Declaration, from the San Remo Peace Conference and from the League of Nations. The Levy Report simply confirmed what was already known decades earlier.

> *After an extensive investigation, we determined that Judea and Samaria were not legally "occupied." It was not under legal control of any entity, including Jordan, whose declaration of sovereignty over the region was never recognized by international organizations like the UN. As a result, building by Israel in Judea and Samaria does not violate the Geneva Convention. In contrast, Israel, as the representative of the Jewish people, can claim a historic right to build in Judea and Samaria. No one can deny this historic right. There are no pacts, treaties, or any other documents that attribute Palestinian rights to the region.[6]*

(Alan Baker, Member of
The Levy Committee, January 2013)

It's certainly relevant to note an interesting side note that Baker shared – he had presented the committee's conclusions to many diplomats, and all accepted them – except for Israel. Why is Israel afraid to assert its national rights?

Refugees – The issue of refugees is one that has stood in the way of every potential peace agreement between Israel and the Palestinian Authority, so once again, we need to ask the question, Why? Why, so many decades after the reestablishment of Israel as a sovereign nation again do we have this seemingly intractable obstacle that should have been resolved so many years ago, when the refugees first fled or were driven out of their native lands?

The United Nations Relief and Works Agency (UNRWA) has defined a Palestine refugee as a person "whose normal place of residence was Palestine between June 1946 and May 1948, who lost both their homes and means of livelihood as a result of the 1948 Arab-Israeli conflict ..." Based on the UNRWA definition, the number of original Palestine refugees has declined from 711,000 in 1950 to an estimated 30 to 50,000 in 2012.[7]

In May 2012, the United States Senate Appropriations Committee approved a definition of a Palestine refugee to include only those original Palestine refugees who were actually displaced between June 1946 and May 1948, resulting in an estimated number of 30,000.[8] That relatively small number is roughly consistent with the actual statistics of the UNRWA report. So what's the big deal? How do we explain the brouhaha every time the peace negotiators mention the refugee problem? Surely, 30,000 refugees could be easily resettled in neighboring Arab countries, could they not?

However, the UNRWA report goes on to create an absurd situation by stating that "The descendants of the original Palestine refugees in the male line are also eligible for registration", and therefore, when we include all of those several generations of descendants who have registered as Palestinians, an estimated 5 million Palestinian refugees are registered in total in 2012.[9] It's a far cry from the original 30,000 and it certainly makes a mockery of the original UNRWA definition of a Palestinian refugee. Could it be that hatred of Jews at that international body has something to do with the twisting of the UN's own history?

The challenge is further compounded if we recognize the reality that the Arab refugees from Israel are not the only Middle Eastern refugees that need to be considered here. The fact is that after the State of Israel was declared in 1948, close to a million Jews were persecuted terribly and were forced to flee their native lands in the Arab world. Countries such as Egypt, Libya, Yemen, Syria, Iraq, Tunisia, Algeria, and Morocco all contributed to this flood of Jewish refugees seeking to escape persecution. There were at least 260,000 Jewish refugees (not counting their descendants) between the years 1948-1951,[10] most of whom were welcomed by their brethren into the newly declared Jewish state. This was despite the fact that the refugees spoke a different language than the newly reestablished mother tongue of Israel. It didn't matter that there were cultural differences or that many of the new immigrants came from distant lands. They were welcomed in as lost family. This contrasted greatly with the cold treatment accorded the 30,000 (note the much smaller number of) Arab refugees from Israel by their brethren in the 20-plus Arab nations who refused to integrate them into their own populations, despite the common language and culture.

One might think that the 260,000 Jewish refugees from Arab/Muslim lands would have been extended the same sympathy from the United Nations as their 30,000 Arab counterparts. As is clear from the historical record, that is not what happened. Disproportionate attention was given to the tiny amount of Arab refugees and frantic attempts were made to multiply their numbers by including their descendants in the new reckoning of the figures. Obviously, to the self-righteous, unbiased denizens of peace at the UN, the hundreds of thousands of children of the Jewish refugees didn't deserve to be counted as refugees, nor did their several million grandchildren, while the so-called Palestinians did. If we judge UNWRA by its own definition of a Palestinian refugee and replace the words Palestine or Palestinian with "one of the Arab/Muslim countries" or "Jew", we see a bigotry that has never been more blatant in that international body:

> *The United Nations Relief and Works Agency (UNRWA)*
> *has defined a Jewish refugee as a person ... whose normal*
> *place of residence was one of the Arab/Muslim countries*
> *between June 1946 and May 1948, who lost both their*
> *homes and means of livelihood as a result of the 1948*
> *Arab-Israeli conflict ... The descendants of the original*
> *Jewish refugees in the male line ... are also eligible for*
> *registration.*

The unfair and discriminatory treatment of the Jewish refugees from Arab/Muslim countries by the international community was far greater than that accorded to the Arab refugees. Anyone who dares to criticize Israel for the "plight of the remaining Palestinian refugees should redirect his/her wrath towards the Arab nations and then go take a course in basic arithmetic, for 30,000 does not come close to equaling 260,000. As the saying goes, those in glass houses should not throw stones. I guess they haven't learned that lesson either.

Land for Peace – Ever since the first Camp David Accords were signed by Menachem Begin and Anwar Sadat, all peace negotiations have been based on the premise that little Israel, a country similar in size to the American state of New Jersey, is required to give up large strategic chunks of its territory to the substantially larger Arab nations in exchange for the promise of peace. The asymmetry in the equation could not be greater and the continued Arab insistence on such an unbalanced exchange shows that their intentions are to weaken Israel to the extent that it won't be able to defend itself. For example, if Israel were to surrender what the Palestinian Authority has been demanding as its minimum demand – namely Judea, Samaria, and the eastern side of Jerusalem – Israel's Ben Gurion International Airport and Tel Aviv would both be within nine miles of enemy missiles. Would a peace treaty be worth such a risk? When signing a peace treaty with an Islamic nation it's critical for Israel to remember the Islamic concept of "hudna", often translated as a truce. Hudna has a distinct meaning in Islam, well-rooted in the teachings of the founder of Islam, Muhammad, who struck a legendary, ten-year hudna with the Quraysh tribe that controlled Mecca in the seventh century. Over the following two years, Mohammad rearmed and took advantage of a minor Quraysh infraction to break the hudna and launch the full conquest of Mecca, the holiest city in Islam.

When Yasser Arafat infamously invoked Muhammad's hudna in 1994 to describe his own Oslo commitments "on the road to Jerusalem," the implication was clear.[11] Arafat was sending a clear signal that when his forces have sufficiently prepared for the next battle, he would find a technical infraction by Israel and use it as an excuse to revert to violence as his longer term strategy against Israel. We see that this is what happened in September of 2000 when Arafat and Fatah launched the second intifada of terrorist warfare against Israeli civilians.

As for Hamas, they have repeatedly proven their commitment to a tactical hudna – replenishing their military strength during the quiet periods, then returning with increased deadliness. As recently documented by The Washington Institute, Hamas agreed to no less than ten ceasefires in the past ten years, and after every single one returned freshly armed for terror. Hundreds of Israeli citizens have paid for these hudnas with their lives.[12]

As we can see, the entire concept of a peace process with an insincere peace partner is fatally flawed and has been from the beginning. Nonetheless, the pressure for the process to continue continues with little thought given to the fact that the same basic mistake is being made over and over again. Israelis are notorious for making repeated "good-will gestures" (usually the release of unrepentant terrorists from prison) to bring the Palestinian Authority back to the negotiating table, but is that a logical tactic in a sensible strategy that has a reasonable chance of working?

For they have healed the hurt of the daughter of my

*people slightly, saying (once again) ... Peace, peace –
when there is no peace.*

(Jeremiah 8:11)

*Insanity is doing the same thing, over and over again,
but expecting different results.[13]*

(Albert Einstein)

The peace process is built on the wrong premise. Perhaps the time has come for those who truly want to see peace between Israel and its neighbors to try an abrupt change of strategy. Instead of land for peace, let's try peace for peace. In other words, the new basic premise would be and should be that if one truly wants a peaceful, harmonious, and productive relationship, it has to be built on mutual respect. Individuals have always understood this in their own interpersonal relationships. No marriage has the possibility of being peaceful and harmonious if there is absolutely no give and take. When one partner repeatedly takes and takes and the other consistently gives and gives, the seeds of eventual if not immediate discord will certainly grow.

There are four character types among people.

One who says ... What's mine is mine and what's yours is yours is of average character.

One who says ... What's mine is yours and what's yours is mine is unlearned.

One who says ... What's mine is yours and what's yours is yours is pious.

One who says ... What's yours is mine and what's mine is mine is wicked.

(Ethics of the Fathers 5:13)

In this tract of ancient Jewish wisdom, we see the healthy element of give and take within the context of mutual respect. The individual of average character understands the concept of mutual respect coupled with self-interest, while the pious one

Peace Through Strength – Economic, Military, and Strategic: *US President Ronald Reagan, shown walking with Israeli Prime Minister Menachem Begin, was ridiculed by many on the left for his belief in good and evil, and even more so, that evil could be defeated through strength. He stood his ground and was proven right when his actions brought about the fall of the Soviet Union and its Communist satellites, what he had called "the evil empire".*

seeks to even rise above it. This applies to roughly equivalent relationships, but what about a situation like Israel's, in which giving its own biblical, historic heartland and minimal strategic depth to those whose very culture is the antithesis of sincerity, giving, and mutual respect could imperil Israel's survival? For Israel to give away concrete assets like land and water in such a situation would be akin to national suicide. Furthermore, for Israel to allow itself to be flooded by a sea of descendants of Arab refugees, while the rights of its much more numerous refugees is totally ignored by the world would be illogical at best.

For that reason, along with an intricate understanding of human psychology, the Torah has always counseled against negotiating with those who are sworn to Israel's destruction. No matter how appealing the allure of peace promises may be

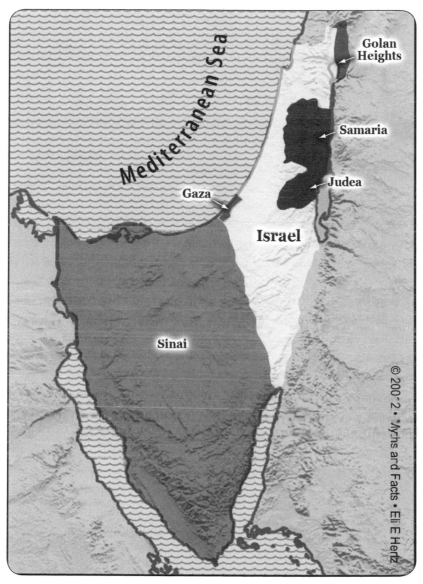

Fruits Of The Six Day War: *We see on this map the area of the State of Israel as of 2012, with the areas of Judea, Samaria, the Golan Heights, Gaza, and Sinai delineated separately. Despite the fact that these areas were captured in a defensive war, Israel has been pressured to surrender some of them in exchange for fleeting promises of peace and normal relations.*

and no matter how painful the immediate suffering of war and terrorism, we are forbidden to raise up the hopes of those who boldly call for peace, but in actuality are seeking to destroy Israel piece by piece until the tiny Jewish state can no longer be defended.

> *You shall not seal a covenant with the inhabitants of this land ... but you have not obeyed My voice.*
>
> (Judges 2:2)

The self-proclaimed pro-Israel liberals, who protest against every single battle and cry tears of joy every time that our deceptive neighbors say the word peace in public have a lot of growing up to do. Like the self-centered child who wants what he wants when he wants it, the peace-mongerers continue their calls for peace negotiations and Israeli land concessions at the very moment in time when Israeli intelligence estimates that at least 100,000 missiles are being pointed at Israeli cities.[14] Such weakness will only bring war to our doorstep faster by encouraging the enemy. As much as we may wish that the Arabs were ready to lay down their arms, we are adults and we need to see the reality for what it is. There will be no peace until the Arabs are prepared to exchange peace for peace – a fair deal. Perhaps when they see that we are strong, both militarily and psychologically, they will be ready for such a peace. American President Ronald Reagan, who defeated the Soviet empire without war and without compromising his principles, said it best:

> *Peace is made by the fact of strength – economic, military, and strategic. Peace is lost when such strength disappears or, just as bad, is seen by an adversary as disappearing.*[15]
>
> (Ronald Reagan, 1980)

> *I hope it will be recorded that I appealed to our best hopes, not our worst fears, to our confidence, rather than*

our doubts, to the facts, not to fantasy ... Hope, confidence, and facts are at the heart of my vision of peace.[16]

(Ronald Reagan, 1980)

Israel will not bring peace by sacrificing its territorial integrity. Israel will not bring peace by succumbing to world pressure. Both of these measures will only show weakness and invite pressure for further concessions, as it has in the past. Last but not least, Israel will not bring peace by betraying its essence, a nation that was founded on biblical principles.

For you shall pass over the Jordan (River) to go in to possess the land that the Lord your God has given you, and you shall possess it and dwell therein.

(Deuteronomy 11:31)

The principle of sole sovereignty for Israel between the Jordan River to the Mediterranean Sea, which of course includes Judea, Samaria, and all of Jerusalem is indisputable, but the prophetic biblical words go much further, implying eventual Israeli sovereignty in what is now the Kingdom of Jordan extending to Iraq, and also in the Sinai Desert, now controlled by the Muslim Brotherhood in Egypt:

Unto your seed have I given this land from the river of Egypt unto the great river, the River Euphrates.

(Genesis 15:18)

How it will all play out over time remains to be seen. I personally don't believe that Israel should attack Jordan or Egypt, but the biblical principles are there to give us guidance when opportunities arise. In the Six Day War of 1967, Israel was given an opportunity and acted on those principles unapologetically in recapturing Judea, Samaria, Jerusalem, Gaza, Sinai, and the Golan Heights. Years later, acting against biblical principles, Israel gave Sinai and Gaza and parts of Judea and Samaria to Egypt and the Palestinian Authority for the promise of peace. Egypt is now controlled by the Muslim Brotherhood and Gaza by Hamas, showing us that we have surrendered material assets and the promise of peace has failed to materialize.

In 1967, we also missed an opportunity. The Temple Mount was in our hands, yet Israeli Defense Minister Moshe Dayan handed it over to the Muslim Wakf, the Jordanian Muslim ruling authority, rather than acting assertively to insure Israeli sovereignty and freedom of religion. Due to that foolish act, it is today forbidden, at the risk of arrest, for a non-Muslim to pray on the Temple Mount. Once again, we are given opportunities and we need to seize the moment when they are presented before us.

In recent years, we have seen the phenomenon of Israel merely reacting to Arab aggression and/or political initiatives, always responding to, but never initiating offensive action. This flawed strategy has prevented Israel from winning its recent conflicts in Gaza and Lebanon, as well as its political battles on the international stage. Even Israel's various peace initiatives are always reactions to American and European Union pressure, and therefore, they don't take Israel's legitimate historical rights and interests into serious consideration.

Perhaps the time has come to take a more proactive approach?

CHAPTER NINE

Does Israel Need A Peace Process?

Several reasons are given by the peace process promoters as to why Israel needs the peace process, not because of public pressure or because of the needs of the so-called Palestinians, but due to Israel's own self-interest. Because we are a little country, we so often react to others, rather than making decisions solely based on our own needs. Many Israelis stress that we need to get rid of Judea and Samaria if we are to survive as a Jewish state. They refer to the threat of Arab demography, specifically the concern that if Israel doesn't allow the creation of an independent Palestinian state in Judea, Samaria, and Gaza, it will soon be overrun by a quickly multiplying Arab population.

> *The womb of the Arab woman is my strongest weapon.*[1]

> (Yasser Arafat, August 13, 2001)

As the line of reasoning goes, most secular, worldly Jews in Tel Aviv and other enlightened Israeli cities don't believe in traditional marriage anymore and if they do, they don't have more than one or two children (plus a cat and a dog). While that might be true on the island of Manhattan, where some 50% of households consist of one person, or in Stockholm Sweden where the figure is 60%[2], in most of Israel that is not at all the case, and patterns are moving in the more traditional direction. Jews in Israel are marrying younger and having larger families.

Nonetheless, there are still some notable doubters in Israel who, perhaps due to the damage that it would cause to their own political agendas, don't want to accept the new facts on the ground.

> *Anyone who believes that Israel can maintain its current hold on all the West Bank is living in a dream.*

The above words were spoken by the feisty Prime Minister Ehud Olmert several years ago, as he addressed a gathering of Jordan Valley (Samarian) farmers.[3] One might think that with the obvious Iranian and Hezbollah threats that had been hanging over Israel's head for years, as well as the ominous Hamas buildup in Gaza, along with the rise of the Muslim Brotherhood and al-Qaeda in the Middle East, Israeli politicians would be placing their focus and concern elsewhere. Nonetheless, the issue of the demographic threat to Israel supposedly caused by its presence in Judea and Samaria periodically returns to the front pages.

In order to judge this issue rationally, avoiding the emotional diatribes frequently launched by those on both sides of the issue, it is crucial to examine the facts. As Olmert rightly has emphasized and his colleagues all across the political spectrum concur, "Everyone understands that the State of Israel can't exist without a Jewish majority." His convergence/realignment plan for unilateral withdrawal from Judea and Samaria was based specifically on this perception, the problematic reality of a tiny Jewish population living among a large and rapidly rising Palestinian Arab population. His argument was that only by relinquishing control of these territories would Israel be able to maintain its Jewish majority. For a long time, this had been the widely accepted solution by many in Israel to the demographic threat, having massive international support, as well. The problem, however, is that this view had usually been accepted with very little questioning and far less analysis.

Yoram Ettinger, who headed the Israeli research team in a

major demographic study carried out in 2005 and has tracked Israel's demographic situation for many years, has pointed out that Israel is not losing the demographic race. He frequently proclaims that "there is no need to retreat from Jewish geography in order to secure Jewish demography."[4] His studies have demonstrated that the demographic argument of those who have advocated Israeli withdrawal from Judea and Samaria, whether unilateral or negotiated with our neighbors is based on a false reading of the actual patterns. The pessimists seem to ignore both the steady high birthrates of the Jewish population in Judea and Samaria and the ongoing and increasing emigration of the Arab population from those areas. Judea and Samaria Arabs have experienced an annual net-emigration since 1950 (e.g. 16,500 in 2010, 17,000 in 2009 and 17,000 in 2008). At the same time, Jews have experienced annual net-immigration (Aliyah) since 1882, boosted by periodical waves of substantial Aliyah, in defiance of the estimates of Israel's often pessimistic demographic establishment.[5] Furthermore, the media rarely notes that the reports of massive Arab population growth have been deliberately exaggerated to serve Arab/Muslim political interests. For example, in 2011, the number of Arabs in Judea and Samaria was inflated by almost 1 million people (1.6 million and not 2.55 million) through the inclusion of nearly 400,000 overseas residents who have been away for over a year, by a double-count of 350,000 ID card-carrying Jerusalem and West Bank Arabs who are counted as Israeli Arabs by Israel and as West Bankers by the Palestinian Authority, etc. A World Bank September 2006 study documents a 32% "inflation" in the number of Palestinian births.[6]

By closing our eyes to these simultaneous trends, we are simply supporting Hamas/Fatah representations of the traditional Islamic taqiyya – deceptions, propaganda and lies, in this case intended to frighten and ultimately destroy the Jewish state by convincing the average Israeli that the demographic war can't possibly be won. In responding to this media war, we need to keep our eyes on the facts. The true demographic threat for Israel is not on the central mountain ridges of Judea and Samaria, but in areas like the northern region of Galilee, with its large and growing Arab majority, or in secular Tel Aviv, where traditional marriage and large families are unfortunately not yet the norm. As Prof. Dan Meyerstein, president of Ariel University, pointed out in late 2007, the birthrate in Judea and Samaria is "crazily higher than the rest of Israel" – 4.4 children (at the time), as opposed to the national average of 2.8.[7] Both figures have increased since then.

No, the real demographic threat for Israel lies not in the "West Bank," but within pre-1967 Israel, where there has been a steady increase in the birthrate, but it's minimal when compared to the Jews of Judea, Samaria, and Jerusalem, where 6, 8, and even 10 children per family is not unusual. The optimistic and idealistic Jewish residents of Judea and Samaria don't need the encouragement of government subsidies to have large families, and the many Jews who emigrate from Israel every year are greatly underrepresented in their numbers. In their large and growing population, they express their belief in both the Jewish past and future by settling the historic heartland of Israel, despite the current overwhelming political pressures to do the opposite. According to Israel's Interior Ministry, there were over 342,000 Jewish residents in Judea and Samaria at the end of 2011, with another 250,000 in the eastern parts of Jerusalem that Israel liberated in the Six Day War of 1967.[8]

Since then, these numbers have continued to grow. Anyone who lives in Judea and Samaria knows that the demand for homes, especially from young couples and families, is much greater than the supply, and the persistent reports and plans of foolish Israeli politicians succumbing to pressure from not so sincere foreign leaders have limited building projects in these areas. However, Jews are voting with their feet. They continue to arrive from all parts of Israel, as well as from abroad, seeking homes in deeply historic places such as Shiloh, Bet El, Hebron, and the Shechem bloc of communities, and many of those who have grown up there continue to stay on after they marry, in whatever housing is available, raising large families and building for the future in those liberated areas. This is the reality on the ground. Yes, Zionism is alive and well in the biblical heartland of Israel, both idealistically and demographically.

The current demographic tailwind should further expand the Jewish majority. From 80,400 births in 1995, the number of Jewish births surged by 56% to 125,500 in 2010, while the annual number of Israeli Arab births has stabilized due to their successful integration into Israel's infrastructures of health, education, employment, finance, medicine, politics, sports and the arts. Israel's Jewish-Arab fertility gap was reduced from six births per woman in 1969 to 0.5 in 2011, trending toward a convergence at three births per woman.

The decline in the West Bank Arab fertility is faster than the decline among Israeli Arabs, resulting from an accelerated urbanization process (from a 70% rural society in 1967 to a 78% urban society in 2011), an expanded education and career mentality among women, reduced teen pregnancy, institutionalized family planning, etc.[9]

Looking at the broader picture, Israel need not fear its demographic future. Despite the fact that the establishment demographers have been warning for years of a return to the Jewish minority status between the Jordan River and the Mediterranean Sea, the current trends say quite the opposite. From a minority of 8% and 33% – west of the Jordan River – in 1900 and 1947 respectively, the six million Jews in Israel have become a solid majority of 66% in 2011, in the combined area of Judea and Samaria (West Bank) and pre-1967 Israel.[10]

Given the data cited above, it seems clear that the demographic threat to Israel's existence is fading with each passing week. Israel is the only part of the world that is out-populating the Muslims. If trends continue, we can expect that the politicians of the Israeli Left will slowly abandon their demographic delusions and will probably seek out other equally unconvincing excuses for surrendering their biblical heartland – which brings us to another one of the self-interest arguments: What is Israel to do when the whole world is demanding the two-state solution, the creation of an independent Palestinian Authority run state in Judea and Samaria? How can Israel as a tiny country refuse the demands of the powerful United States of America?

To properly understand this fundamental question that really digs to the core of Zionism, we need some historical perspective. The basic common sense seems to tell us that little Israel cannot dare to defy the United States nor the European Union, countries with far more political and economic clout, not to mention population and land mass. An Israel that refuses the two-state solution, the establishment of a Palestinian state alongside Israel, is standing alone against world opinion, which would seem to be the epitome of self-destructive behavior.

However, Israel is not just another little country seeking to curry favor with the giants. For 2000 years, Jews were forced to show allegiance to and request kindness from the Muslim and Christian rulers in the countries in which they dwelled, often accepting official second-class (Dhimmi in Islam) status and constantly looking over their shoulders with concern about their status or safety. The modern State of Israel was reestablished out of these dark shadows of persecution including massacres, pogroms, forced conversions, and expulsions, culminating in the Holocaust murder of six million Jews by Nazi Germany. The rise of the State of Israel was intended to put an end to the helplessness of the wandering Jew. The new sovereign nation back in its land would welcome in all of its refugees and would stand proudly in defense of Jewish rights in Israel, in the Middle East, and around the world.

What matters is not what the Goyim (non-Jews) say, but what the Jews do.[11]

(First Israeli Prime Minister David Ben-Gurion)

The term "Goyim" literally means nations, but in general use refers to nations other than Israel. Did Ben-Gurion's statement mean that the newly reestablished State of Israel would ignore the appeals and the concerns of friendly nations like the United States? Certainly not, but it does mean that when Israel is faced with existential decisions or any other decisions of Zionist principle, any Israeli leader that succumbs to foreign dictat is severely lacking a sense of national responsibility. Therefore in 1948, after a successful battle against Arab invading armies, Ben-Gurion was pressured to retreat. Despite the relative weakness of Israel at that time, he refused the diplomatic onslaught. Likewise, when Prime Minister Golda Meir was pressured by US President Richard Nixon to retreat to the 1949 armistice line and redivide Jerusalem, she responded proactively by not only refusing Nixon's demands, but by building new Jewish neighborhoods in formerly Jordanian-occupied parts of the city. Prime Minister Levi Eshkol followed the same principle, building the Jerusalem neighborhood that came to be called Ramot Eshkol, despite pressure to halt Jewish building

The Best Defense Is A Good Offense: *Despite pressure from US President Richard Nixon to withdraw to the 1949 armistice lines, Israeli Prime Minister Golda Meir refused, instead moving forward by building new Jewish neighborhoods in formerly Jordanian-occupied parts of Jerusalem.*

in the areas of the capital that had been liberated in 1967.

Even beyond Israel's borders, the psychological principle remained the same. On June 7, 1981, Prime Minister Menachem Begin defied American opposition and Israel launched a lightning strike on the Tammuz nuclear reactor that was nearing operational weapons level capacity in Iraq. The attack was roundly criticized by most countries, including the United States, and Israel was condemned in two separate UN resolutions, but Begin went forward because the national interest was at stake.[12] The world is now a safer place because of it.

Almost a decade later, Prime Minister Yitzchak Shamir, short in stature, but as tough as nails, openly disagreed with senior US officials, bluntly telling then-Secretary of State

Short In Stature, But As Tough As Nails: *Prime Minister Yitzchak Shamir was perhaps disliked by some American politicians, but he was respected for his toughness and his principles. His concessions under pressure were few and were usually based on a calculation that such a concession would be in Israel's interest without surrendering any concrete assets.*

James Baker, "Mr. Secretary, you can demand what you choose to demand, but this is our country and we will not agree to do anything that will harm its interests and future even if demanded by our best friend." US Senate leaders George Mitchell and Bob Dole later told Shamir, "You know why we respect you despite our disagreements with your policies? Because you're tough!"[13] Shamir greatly expanded the settlement enterprise in Judea and Samaria over American objections, because the national interest was seen as first and foremost.

Was there an increase in tensions with the American and other administrations as a result of Israel standing firm in each of these instances? Yes, there was, but the foundation of that relationship was strong enough that in the long term, Israel was respected for standing by its principles. A strong ally is considered reliable and is respected by his firmness, by his strength, and by his unwillingness to cave in to pressure. When Israel has collapsed under American pressure, as at Camp David or at Wye Plantation, or has shown the weakness of withdrawal, as in the Oslo Accords or at Gush Katif in 2005, it has increased the demands imposed on it exponentially, making a peaceful resolution a near impossibility. On the other hand, when Israel has stayed the course, sticking calmly but firmly to its Zionist, Jewish principles, the respect is not long in coming.

An Israel that is on the rise as a technological and economic power need not cringe every time a foreign politician blinks. An Israel that is demographically, economically, militarily, and technologically strong is a tremendous asset at the strategic intersection of three continents. The United States has gained enormously from Israel, even just in intelligence information alone,[14] as its sole reliable ally in a Middle East controlled increasingly by Islamic fundamentalists.

The United States has been weakened by the neo-European approach of the Obama administration of pandering to the Islamic world while distancing the US from Israel. The forces of Jihad will continue to rise in the Middle East and in the West

Israeli Weakness At Wye: *Prime Minister Netanyahu, seen here with Foreign Minister Madelaine Albright and PA President Yasser Arafat at the Wye Plantation summit. Israeli land for peace concessions, like those agreed to by Netanyahu at Wye, have almost always brought more terrorism in their wake, just the opposite of the stated purpose of such retreats.*

as the Obama administration continues to boost the Muslim Brotherhood as a legitimate partner and ally, but eventually Americans will realize that the Islamic fundamentalists are not only taking over the Middle East. Their sights are on North America, but the Americans, who are so busy fighting each other over social issues like gay marriage and abortion will suddenly notice that those important issues have been overrun by an Islamic tsunami. Muslims are the fastest growing population in America. As there are now 15-25% Muslim populations in many European cities, this horror movie is being funded and exported to the United States from the Middle East and it's already showing at many theaters in Michigan and in hundreds of Islamic charter schools throughout the United States where Jihad is a central part of the curriculum.[15] America's Islamic population – due to immigration and the high birth rates of Muslim women – is increasing at a rate of 6% per year. This demographic, verified by Allied Media Corp and the World Almanac, shows that America's Islamic population will double by 2014 and triple by 2020.[16]

At some point, and perhaps sooner than we think, Americans will wake up to see that the free America that they once loved has been transformed and they will frantically seek solutions, but it will be too late.

Israel's vital role as an island of stability and advocacy for the free world will finally be recognized as the turmoil of the Arab Spring continues in the years to come. If Americans somehow rediscover their role as the bastion of freedom and liberty and as a Judeo-Christian civilization, they will need the partnership of an Israel that increasingly stands for family values and private initiative in the midst of a sea of fundamentalist Islamic domination. Whether or not that partnership is strengthened, Israel needs to move forward according to its very own Zionistic, biblically-based principles, without excessive concern for what the nations will say. And that is also the correct path to peace.

CHAPTER TEN

Peace For Peace: Moving Forward

We, the German Fuhrer and Chancellor, and the British Prime Minister, have had a further meeting today and are agreed in recognizing that the question of Anglo-German relations is of the first importance for our two countries and for Europe ... We regard the agreement signed last night and the Anglo-German Naval Agreement as symbolic of the desire of our two peoples never to go to war with one another again ... My good friends, for the second time in our history, a British Prime Minister has returned from Germany bringing peace with honor. I believe it is "peace in our time." Go home and get a nice quiet sleep.[1]

(British Prime Minister, Neville Chamberlain, September 1938)

We all know how that story ended up. Six million Jews later, we should have learned our lesson and in future reports of peace in our time, checked not just messenger, but also the content of the message.

Well, he's surrounded by pacifists who all want peace
They pray for it nightly that the bloodshed must cease
Now, they wouldn't hurt a fly. To hurt one they would weep
They lay and they wait for this bully to fall asleep
He's the neighborhood bully.[2]

(Bob Dylan, "Neighborhood Bully", 1983)

One More Peace Summit Going Nowhere: *US Secretary of State Hillary Rodham Clinton at negotiations between the Palestinians and Israelis in Sharm el-Sheikh, Egypt in 2010, hosted by President Hosni Mubarak, and joined by Palestinian President Mahmoud Abbas and Israeli Prime Minister Benjamin Netanyahu.*

The biting irony of Bob Dylan's words about Israel (the so-called neighborhood bully) and its self-righteous neighbors couldn't be more accurate. It is one thing to make peace with true pacifists who only want to live in harmony. It is quite another to believe the deceptive cries of the sanctimonious leftists and their Islamic cohorts, who quickly gather in panic to stop any Israeli attempts at defending its citizens. The world is happy to show sympathy for Israel as it buries its dead, but if it fights back and maybe even has a chance of winning? Then it is instantly transformed, in the world's eyes, from victim to neighborhood bully.

Case in Point: Gaza, November of 2012, Israel's planned (and long-awaited) Gaza ground operation against Hamas was aborted due to the heavy international pressure for a ceasefire, which Prime Minister Netanyahu and his cabinet agreed to before the ground operation had even commenced. As tens of thousands of Israeli soldiers, including thousands of reservists, were called to the Gaza region to put an end to eight years of Hamas missiles being fired on Israeli cities and towns, President Muhammad Morsi of Muslim Brotherhood-dominated Egypt called for "an end to the farce of Israeli aggression,"[3] while Turkish President and close Obama confidant Recep Tayyip Erdogan called Israel a "terrorist state,"[4] and all of this in the name of peace. US Secretary of State Hillary Clinton rushed to Israel to attain a quick ceasefire and prevent Israel's ground operation, all the while proclaiming her commitment to Israel's security. The ceasefire that was eventually reached with Egyptian mediation was achieved mainly through the Obama administration, because Egypt had refused any direct contact with Israel, but Egypt was nonetheless given the primary role as arbiter and verifier of the agreement. The absurdity of such an arrangement was apparently overlooked by Israel's pusillanimous leadership, which heaped abundant praise on the peace efforts of Morsi, the Muslim Brotherhood leader who had just saved his Muslim brother Hamas from annihilation.

We have seen this pattern too many times – in the Lebanon War in 1982, when Israel had downed 86 Syrian planes in just the first week[5] of the war; and in the first Gaza conflict in 2009, when Israel was in the middle of a successful ground operation against Hamas and Islamic Jihad terrorists – in both instances, the frantic international pressure was applied to force a ceasefire, lest Israel actually win a clear-cut victory and dictate the terms of a truce. In such circumstances, the world leaders and diplomats immediately go into full gear to prevent Israel from winning decisively.

However, it is perhaps too simple to blame the world for our failures. An Israel lacking belief in the justice of its cause, and therefore, nervous about asserting its legitimate sovereignty rights against world pressure, has caved in repeatedly, thereby inviting the pressure upon itself. With each premature ceasefire agreement, we are simply kicking the proverbial can down the road for a few more years each time, until the enemy fully refuels its weapons supply. After the 2012 Gaza ceasefire agreement was finalized, as Israel's political leadership was trying to put a positive spin on its obvious lack of political courage, Hamas stressed its consensus opinion, that the agreement had not called for an end to the smuggling of weapons,[6] and therefore, the Hamas arms smuggling/refueling process would continue unabated, in preparation for the next war. Hudna in action, once again.

To sign naive peace agreements with those who talk about peace, but who adhere to an ideology that seeks to destroy, dominate, and dispossess; that is indeed the definition of suicidal actions. The religious justification for lying and deception, taqiyya, voids the trustworthiness of the Islamic signers of any peace deals and renders any signed agreement worthless.

That being the case, is there a way that everyone's favorite peace process can work?

Everybody sees a difficulty in the question of relations between Arabs and Jews. But not everybody sees that there is no solution to this question. No solution! There is a gulf, and nothing can bridge it ... We, as a nation, want this country to be ours; the Arabs, as a nation, want this country to be theirs.[7]

(David Ben-Gurion, June 1919
as quoted in Time magazine, July 24, 2006)

No solution at all? I disagree. Perhaps there is no solution that both sides will happily agree to, but there are just and historically correct solutions that Israel can apply, if need be, unilaterally. The problem has been that the peace-pushers are always looking for the magical peace plan that will prevent future conflict, while simultaneously satisfying the Islamic goal of shrinking Israel into a greatly weakened, almost defenseless state. Virtually every peace plan that has been proposed since the reestablishment of the Jewish state has been based on the flawed land for peace concept, and therefore, none of the solutions that have been bandied about in recent years have had any serious chance of succeeding, but that doesn't mean that there is no solution or genuine peace plan that can work. Almost every peace plan that has been proposed has been unrealistic because the various peace architects have ignored the historical lessons of Israel's past wars and conflicts with its neighbors. "Give peace a chance" may have been a nice slogan for John Lennon and Yoko Ono in the time of the Vietnam War, but if we truly want to have a peace that will last in the Middle East, we need to have a peace plan that derives its guidance from Israel's history, both modern and ancient.

We are living in an age of secular skepticism, bordering on arrogance, toward the very biblical principles that are Israel's heritage, but that Israel has shared with the nations of the world. Due to the secular knee-jerk skepticism, we have accepted the legitimacy of the term political correctness, a term which essentially describes the dogmatism of the far Left ideologues that ridicules any reference to biblical principles to justify a political position. In other words, it's okay to quote left-wing American Jewish actors like Ed Asner[8] and Mandy Patinkin[9] to support a blatantly anti-Israel political position, but God forbid that Jews of substance, like the biblical heroes Moses or Joshua should be cited as sources of guidance!

> *How long will you wait before coming to take possession of the land that the Lord, God of your fathers has given you?*
>
> (Joshua 18:3)

Just as the biblical principles and relevant commentaries teach us how to lead a healthy, moral life in marriage and family, so, too, they provide clear instruction for how to fight wars and how to create peace in Israel and around the world. Any peace process that is not based on those principles is doomed to failure. I say this not just because I believe in those principles, but because history has proven that the alternative doesn't work. Nonetheless, we continue to bang our heads against the wall trying to put the proverbial square peg in the round circle of

(Israeli) land for (Arab insincere promises of) peace, and then we wonder why it doesn't work.

Any successful peace plan can only be based on peace for peace – no more Israeli surrender of precious, scarce land – and no negotiating away our vital assets in order to tell that unsympathetic world that we compromised with our enemies. Compromise is not the solution to every conflict of nations and in the case of Israel and its enemies, it certainly hasn't worked.

> *You shall not seal a covenant with the inhabitants of this land ... but you did not listen to My voice.*
>
> (Judges 2:2)

> *Discussions of autonomy plans are just a prelude to surrendering parts of the Land of Israel – and not just small territories – but rather large expansive parts such as Judea, Samaria, Gaza, Hebron, and Jerusalem etc. This involves life-and-death issues! As has been stated,* ***it is irrelevant what the Jews think or say, and how they interpret it. What matters is how the gentiles understand it.*** *They interpret the plan as one eventually leading to the surrender of parts of the Land of Israel and the establishment of a Palestinian state* [10]
>
> (Rabbi Menachem Mendel Schneerson,
> The Lubavitcher Rebbe, January 1992)

Aside from the biblical and psychological angles cited above, there is simply no logical reason to sign Camp David and Oslo-style peace agreements with our Islamic enemies, agreements that are patently flimsy and unreliable, as we have seen in the Muslim Brotherhood and Salafist takeover of the Egyptian government in that country or in the much earlier overthrow of the Shah of Iran.

Furthermore, I, for one, will not play this silly but dangerous game of ignoring the reality of Islamic taqiyya, or deception, nor will I base my approach to peace on wishful, delusionary thinking.

Too many young lives have been lost just in my own neighborhood as a result of such irresponsible behavior on the part of Israel's political leadership.

It's time for a change, but I'm not speaking here about a change in political faces or names.

It's time for a conceptual change in how we approach peace and how we develop peace plans.

My proposed plan, which I am calling *Peace for Peace* is a realistic peace plan in which Israel takes its destiny into its own hands, **based on eternal, historical truths** that Israel has known for thousands of years and that have been adopted by Western civilization.

Let us be clear: A peace plan that has a chance of working needs to include the following essential statements of principle:

1. The land of Israel is the eternal God-given inheritance of the people of Israel. The hope for a peaceful two-state solution is a dangerous desert mirage that will not happen and it's time we stopped raising false hopes. The 20-plus Arab/Muslim states exist on a land mass more than 500 times that of present-day Israel. Israel cannot and should not be expected to surrender any more land.

2. There can be only a one-state solution in the land of Israel with Israel as the only sovereign nation in that one state. The Arabs/Muslims have more than enough nations/states in their sovereign possession to serve the economic and social needs of their populations. If we examine the biblical principles, the boundaries of Israel may eventually extend to the Nile River in Egypt, into southern and central Lebanon in the north and to the Euphrates River in the east. The current Kingdom of Jordan is included within those potential borders, as well.

*To your descendants I have given this land, from the
river of Egypt to the great river, the Euphrates River.*
(Genesis 15:18)

*Every place upon which the sole of your foot will tread,
I have given to you.*

(Joshua 1:3)

Do the borders proscribed in the Bible mean that Israel
should immediately attack and take control of parts of Jordan,
Lebanon, or Egypt? Is this a call for the immediate invasion of
sovereign nations? No, the above border descriptions were not
cited to encourage constant expansionism, but to fully understand
the legitimate geographic rights of the people of Israel.

The biblical, historical rights are clear and were reaffirmed
by the United Kingdom's Foreign Secretary Lord Arthur James
Balfour and the British Mandate over what was then known as
Palestine in the Balfour Declaration in 1917.[11] How, if, and/
or when the nation of Israel exercises those complete rights is
a separate issue. In Judaism, there are two concepts that help
to guide us in practical day to day decisions in a world that is
far from the ideal – the concepts of L'Chatchila, which means
doing things the right way from the start and B'Diavad, which
means managing with a situation as it is, after the fact. In other
words, it would have been better if Israel had taken possession
of the entire land of Israel in 1948, and not given parts of it
away in recent years, but that not being the case, Israel must
at least declare its absolute sovereignty over all the land that is
currently in its possession. This includes officially annexing all
of the land from the Mediterranean Sea to the Jordan River and
unapologetically applying Israeli law to all of these areas. With
the instabilities in the Islamic world, I fully expect that there
will at some stage be conflicts with Egypt, Jordan, Syria, and
Lebanon. Most likely, and as always, those conflicts will not
have been initiated by Israel, but Israel will then be presented
with opportunities as a nation under attack and it will be up to

us to seize the moment and repossess those lands, as well. On the other hand, if those countries prefer to establish a status quo of peace for peace, Israel will be happy to accept the offer as long as there is true reciprocity of relations.

3. As a result of the Palestinian Authority action of officially and unilaterally turning to the United Nations for recognition as an independent state of Palestine, an action that was a blatant violation of the Oslo Accords, as is the PA's ongoing monetary and other support for terrorism, Israel will hereby declare the Oslo Accords null and void. All autonomy-related arrangements with the PA will be ended and the PA will cease to be a recognized entity.

4. If the relevant nations of origin agree, the refugee problem will be resolved by a symbolic monetary compensation agreement between Israel and the relevant Arab nations. Both Jewish and Arab refugees will be compensated if they can prove that they personally were born in and lived in the country of origin. Descendents of those refugees will not be compensated. The compensation will be given by the nation of origin, hopefully with funds contributed as well by the international community, which has expressed its concern that this issue be resolved.

5. A path to loyal Israeli citizenship needs to be established for all residents of Israel, including those people presently residing in Judea and Samaria as non-citizens. While the ideal situation would have precluded giving full citizenship to Arab/Muslim haters of Israel, we have to work with an existing situation in which Israeli Arabs in pre-1967 Israel already have full citizenship rights, and therefore, we cannot have a situation of a double standard for those who live in Judea and

Samaria. However, Israel cannot be expected to take in new citizens who are not loyal to the Jewish state.

6. The solution to this challenge is to have an intensive loyal citizenship training course for those who want to acquire membership in the Jewish state. The two-year course will include biblical and modern Zionist history, Jewish religion (there is no separation of synagogue and state in Israel), learning principles of self-sacrifice for the land and people of Israel, and approved volunteerism. Only those residents who commit to perform three years of military or other national patriotic service to the State of Israel at the course's conclusion will be approved to take the final exam. At the end ceremony of the course, the prospective citizen will place a hand on a Tanach, the Hebrew Bible of Israel, and an oath/declaration of loyalty will be made to the State of Israel. If the national service requirement isn't fulfilled within five years, the citizenship will be revoked.

7. Israel need not fear this process, amid concerns that the country will be overrun by hundreds of thousands of hostile Arab Muslim citizens. As we discussed earlier, the demographic ghost no longer is hovering over the Jewish state as the Jewish population continues to grow at a brisk pace. Furthermore, it is far from certain that the offer of this path to loyal citizenship will be accepted. As we have seen in eastern Jerusalem, which has been under Israeli law and sovereignty for many years, but which does not have this rigorous citizenship attainment process in place, many Arabs would refuse the option of Israeli citizenship. If they did, the blame for their stateless status would lie solely with them. They could run to complain to the media or to the UN about their self-inflicted plight, but Israel would offer all such stateless residents the option of free one-way

transportation to one of the neighboring Arab countries, where perhaps they would be happier with their brethren in a culturally similar environment. A one-time stipend would be provided to assist them in the transition.

8. The offer of optional subsidized transfer to another country will be on the table for one year. If that offer is refused, only a very limited number of non-citizens will be allowed to remain. This decision will be based on Israel's needs. The other non-citizens will be expelled to one of the neighboring countries or to any other country that is interested in absorbing them.

If you do not drive out the inhabitants of the land before you, those that remain shall be pins in your eyes and thorns in your sides and they will harass you upon the land in which you dwell.

(Numbers 33:55)

Anyone who doubts the moral soundness and/or legal legitimacy of such a population transfer should learn the history of Europe post-WWII, when millions of residents were forcibly transferred across borders by the victorious Allies for the sake of internal peace between peoples. In the case of Israel, it will have been even more justified from a moral standpoint, as Israel will have offered alternative arrangements first. Only after those magnanimous arrangements are refused, will the forcible transfer option kick in.

9. Israel calls on all sovereign nations in the region to establish cooperative diplomatic relations on the basis of "peace for peace" with Israel. Israel will respect the territorial integrity of those nations in its current form, on the condition that those nations respect the territorial integrity of Israel in its current form.

10. The nation of Israel, that has made the desert bloom

again in our time and has used its culture of learning to become an agricultural and technological giant despite its tiny size, can bring the blessings of peace and prosperity to all of the Middle East. Israel extends its hand in peace to each of its neighbors and to all nations to establish mutually constructive trade relations for mutually beneficial purpose.

I have given you for a covenant to the people, as a light unto the nations ...

(Isaiah 42:6)

While there is no guarantee that the nations of the world will accept the vision of *Peace for Peace*, along with Israel's outstretched hand at this time, the offer of true peace needs to be on the table and extended to all nations.

When a man's ways please the Lord, even his enemies will make peace with him.

(Proverbs 16:7)

By being an example of goodness in our personal and family lives, by sharing our disproportionate scientific and technological accomplishments with other friendly nations, and by constantly extending our hand in unconditional peace, we can ultimately bring lasting peace between Israel, its neighbors and the world.

For from Zion will the Torah spread outward and the word of God from Jerusalem. He will judge among the nations, and will settle the arguments of many peoples. They will beat their swords into plowshares and their spears into pruning hooks; nation will not lift sword against nation and they will study war no more.

(Isaiah 2:3-4)

**May this prophecy of peace
be fulfilled, speedily and in our lifetimes!**

Acknowledgments

No book project is complete without thanking those who made it happen. In this case, I will be concise:

Thank you to my friend, Reuven Kantor, for urging me to write the definitive book about the peace process, especially in light of the recent turmoil confronting Israel in the Middle East.

Thank you to my editor and pre-press director, Chaim Mazo, for organization, calmness under pressure, and insisting that we ignore deadlines when necessary.

Thank you to Joseph Stern, whose dedicated organizational work for the Shiloh Israel Children's Fund frees up some of my time for writing.

Thank you to my wife, Lisa, who enables me to sit at my computer writing when I could be doing other important things at home.

Thank you to the Almighty G-d of Israel, from whose goodness and mercy the ultimate peace will emerge.

Credits

Source Notes

CHAPTER ONE

1. "Imagine". Song by John Lennon (released October 24, 1975)
2. http://www.grunt.com/corps/quotes/3/
3. http://www.ajc.org/site/apps/nlnet/content2.aspx?b=849241&c=ij ITI2PHKoG&ct=4508009
4. http://www.yeshiva.org.il/midrash/shiur.asp?id=4877 , http://www.tapuz.co.il/forums2008/viewmsg.aspx?forumid=102&messageid=144751969
5. http://www.etzion.org.il/vbm/archive/11-jeru/13mikdaoh.rtf
6. http://en.wikipedia.org/wiki/Spoils_system
7. http://www.bobdylan.com/us/songs/neighborhood-bully
8. http://en.wikiquote.org/wiki/David_Ben-Gurion
9. Speaking to the Israel Policy Forum in the USA in June of 2005
10. Speaking at Bar-Ilan University – June 14, 2009
11. http://www.israelnationalnews.com/News/News.aspx/100794
12. ibid
13. Twain, Mark. "The Innocents Abroad.", 1869.
14. http://www.zionism-israel.com/dic/Haj_Amin_El_Husseini.htm
    http://en.wikipedia.org/wiki/Haj_Amin_al-Husseini
    Schwanitz 2008 citing Abd al-Karim al-Umar (ed.), Memoirs of the Grand Mufti, Damascus, 1999, p.126
15. ibid
16. http://www.theisraelproject.org/site/apps/nl/content2.asp?c=hsJP K0PIJpH&b=883997&ct=4687261
17. http://www.mythsandfacts.com/conflict/10/resolution-242.pdf
18. ibid.
19. ibid.
20. ibid.
21. Der Spiegel, November 5, 1969.

CHAPTER TWO

1. http://www.palwatch.org/main.aspx?fi=505
2. ibid
3. ibid
4. http://www.cbn.com/cbnnews/insideisrael/2011/September/ Jerusalem-Dateline-Palestinian-State-vs-Israels-Survival/
5. http://en.wikipedia.org/wiki/Judea_and_Samaria_Area
6. Kook, Rabbi Avraham Yitzchak HaCohen. "Orot HaTeshuva", Or Etzion Publishing House, Mercaz Shapira, Israel.
7. Rubin, David. *The Islamic Tsunami*, Shiloh Israel Press, 2010, pp.152-154.
8. http://www.cbsnews.com/stories/2004/11/12/opinion/main655409. shtml
9. http://www.quotatio.com/topics/humanity.html
10. http://www.foxnews.com/politics/2011/12/10/gingrich-describes-palestinian-people-as-invented/
11. http://www.youtube.com/watch?v=uZJsq_hdlBU
12. http://thehill.com/blogs/blog-briefing-room/news/190457-cain-push-by-so-called-palestinian-people-for-statehood-result-of-obama-weakness
13. http://www.snydertalk.com/?page_id=2760
14. http://www.time.com/time/specials/2007/article/0,28804,1644149_ 1644147_1644129,00.html
15. http://www.iris.org.il/quotes/joburg.htm
16. http://articles.latimes.com/1994-05-19/news/mn-59639_1_peace-process
17. http://en.wikipedia.org/wiki/List_of_Palestinian_suicide_attacks
18. http://www.timesofisrael.com/netanyahu-shamir-was-right-in-criticism-of-arabs
19. http://www.nytimes.com/2010/06/02/opinion/02oz.html?_r=1
20. http://en.wikipedia.org/wiki/Sudetenland
21. http://www.mfa.gov.il/MFA/Peace+Process/ Guide+to+the+Peace+Process/THE+ISRAELI-PALESTINIAN+INTERIM+AGREEMENT.htm
22. http://www.israelnationalnews.com/News/News.aspx/139574
23. http://www.guardian.co.uk/world/2007/may/09/usa.israel

24. http://www.haaretz.com/news/diplomacy-defense/peres-israel-can-t-make-mideast-peace-with-open-eyes-we-must-forget-the-past.premium-1.440157
25. http://en.wikipedia.org/wiki/Wye_River_Memorandum
26. http://en.wikipedia.org/wiki/Ehud_Barak
27. http://worldnews.nbcnews.com/_news/2012/11/23/15357759-what-gaza-fighting-taught-israel-about-possible-war-with-iran?lite
28. http://www.globalpolitician.com/print.asp?id=4782
29. http://en.wikipedia.org/wiki/2000_Camp_David_Summit

CHAPTER THREE

1. http://thinkexist.com/quotations/peace/3.html
2. http://www.history.com/speeches/chamberlain-secures-peace-in-our-time#chamberlain-secures-peace-in-our-time
3. http://en.wikipedia.org/wiki/Paris_Peace_Accords
4. http://en.wikipedia.org/wiki/Camp_David_Accords
5. Gorenberg, Gershom. *The Accidental Empire: Israel and the Birth of the Settlements, 1967-1977*, Henry Holt & Company 2006 pp.220-222.
6. Shlaim, Avi. *The Iron Wall: Israel and the Arab World*, Penguin Books 2001 p.317.
7. http://www.israelnationalnews.com/News/News.aspx/149448
8. http://en.wikipedia.org/wiki/2000_Camp_David_Summit
9. Bob Kemper, "Bush pushes, Sharon digs in", Chicago Tribune, June 27, 2001
10. ibid
11. http://www.jewishvirtuallibrary.org/jsource/Peace/cd2000art.html
12. http://www.time.com/time/world/article/0,8599,2051173,00.html
13. ibid
14. ibid
15. http://en.wikipedia.org/wiki/2000_Camp_David_Summit
16. ibid
17. http://www.jewishvirtuallibrary.org/jsource/Peace/cd2000art.html
18. ibid

CHAPTER FOUR

1. http://www.mfa.gov.il/MFA/Terrorism-+Obstacle+to+Peace/ Palestinian+terror+since+2000/Victims+of+Palestinian+Viol ence+and+Terrorism+sinc.htm
2. http://www.palwatch.org/main.aspx?fi=157&doc_id=1133
3. http://www.imra.org.il/story.php3?id=10457
4. http://tech.mit.edu/V113/N61/rushdie.61n.html
5. http://www.datehookup.com/content-understanding-emotional-abuse.htm
6. Rubin, David. *God, Israel, & Shiloh*, Shiloh Israel Press, 207, 2011. Rubin, David. *The Islamic Tsunami*, Shiloh Israel Press, 2010.
7. Matthew Kalman, USA Today, March 14, 2002.
8. Charles A. Radin, Boston Globe Online, December 4, 2001.
9. http://www.imra.org.il/story.php3?id=11804
10. ibid
11. http://www.jewishvirtuallibrary.org/jsource/Terrorism/PATerror. html
12. ibid
13. http://www.haaretz.com/blogs/east-side-story/thanks-to-al-jazeera-the-mystery-of-arafat-s-death-may-finally-be-cracked-1.448790
14. http://www.wnd.com/2005/09/32263/
15. http://www.haaretz.com/blogs/east-side-story/thanks-to-al-jazeera-the-mystery-of-arafat-s-death-may-finally-be-cracked-1.448790
16. http://en.wikipedia.org/wiki/ Israel's_unilateral_disengagement_plan
17. http://www.washingtonpost.com/wp-dyn/content/ article/2006/01/26/AR2006012600372.html
18. http://www.haaretz.com/news/gaza-settlement-era-ends-with-netzarim-evacuation-1.167590
19. Jerusalem Post, January 3, 2006
20. "Boomerang", Ofer Shelach and Raviv Drucker, Keter Books, 2005 (Hebrew)
21. http://www.ynetnews.com/articles/0,7340,L-4137243,00.html
22. http://en.wikipedia.org/wiki/Mahmoud_Abbas
23. ibid

24. Official PA daily Al-Hayat Al-Jadida, April 15, 2011.
25. Jerusalem Post, May 20, 2011.
26. Life and the Market, supplement to Al-Hayat Al-Jadida, June 19, 2011.
27. http://cnsnews.com/news/article/us-engagement-syria-timeline

CHAPTER FIVE

1. http://www.haaretz.com/weekend/week-s-end/shimon-peres-israeli-idol-1.229351
2. http://www.youtube.com/watch?v=9WlqW6UCeaY
3. http://www.hudson.org/files/pdf_upload/saudi_textbooks_final.pdf
4. ibid
5. ibid
6. ibid
7. http://en.wikipedia.org/wiki/Muhammad
8. http://prophetofdoom.net/article.aspx?g=402&i=4222046 http://www.icbwayland.org/outreach/Muhammad.html http://www.islaam.ca/downloads/Muhammad.pdf
9. Federer, William. J. "What Every American Needs to Know About the Qur'an – A History of Islam & the United States." St. Louis: AmeriSearch Inc., January 2007.
10. ibid
11. Rubin, David. *The Islamic Tsunami*, Jerusalem, Israel. Shiloh Israel Press, 2010.
12. ibid
13. http://usatoday30.usatoday.com/news/world/iraq/2005-05-04-pleasure-marriage_x.htm
14. http://edition.cnn.com/2009/WORLD/asiapcf/10/26/ctw.afghanistan.sex.trade/
15. http://www.somalilandtimes.net/sl/2010/417/32.shtml
16. http://allaboutmuhammad.com/holy-jihad.html
17. http://www.al-islam.org/discovering-islam/13.htm
18. http://allaboutmuhammad.com/holy-jihad.html
19. ibid
20. San Ramon Valley Herald report of a speech to California Muslims in July 1998; quoted in Daniel Pipes' NY Post article, CAIR: Moderate Friends of Terror, Apr. 22, 2002.

21. http://allaboutmuhammad.com/holy-jihad.html
22. http://www.islam-watch.org/Others/Does-Sharia-Promote-Human-Rights.htm
23. http://thomasjoscelyn.blogspot.co.il/2006/02/hamas-hezbollah-ideology-does-not.html
24. http://www.jpost.com/LandedPages/PrintArticle.aspx?id=241826
25. http://www.jpost.com/MiddleEast/Article.aspx?id=263328
26. http://www.israelnationalnews.com/News/Flash.aspx/249791
27. http://palwatch.org/main.aspx?fi=157&doc_id=6854
28. http://www.jpost.com/MiddleEast/Article.aspx?id=200935
29. http://palwatch.org/main.aspx?fi=157&doc_id=6854
30. ibid
31. http://www.cbsnews.com/video/watch/?id=7420664n
32. Benson, Michael T. *Harry S. Truman and the Founding of Israel*. Praeger Publishers, 1997, 190-191.
33. ibid, 190.

CHAPTER SIX

1. http://www.thereligionofpeace.com/Quran/011-taqiyya.htm
2. http://www.motherjones.com/politics/2012/09/romney-secret-video-israeli-palestinian-middle-east-peace
3. Gary DeMar. "America's 200 Year War with Islamic Terrorism – The Strange Case of the Treaty of Tripoli", www.AmericanVision.org
4. Federer, William. J. "What Every American Needs to Know About the Qur'an – A History of Islam & the United States." St. Louis: AmeriSearch Inc., January 2007.
5. http://en.wikipedia.org/wiki/Hudna
6. Federer, William. J. *What Every American Needs to Know About the Qur'an – A History of Islam & the United States*, St. Louis, AmeriSearch Inc., January 2007.
7. ibid
8. ibid
9. http://abcnews.go.com/Blotter/hasan-multiple-mail-accountsofficials/story?id=9065692
10. Anwar al Awlaki.com, November 9, 2009.
11. Interview – Reported by Paula Newton, CNN, January 10, 2010.

12. http://www.palwatch.org/main.aspx?fi=157&doc_id=7284
13. ibid
14. ibid
15. Al-Hayat Al-Jadida, October 26, 2010
16. Federer, William J. "America's God and Country: Encyclopedia of Quotations." St. Louis, Amerisearch, 2000: Pp.10-11.
17. http://www.leaderu.com/orgs/cdf/onug/franklin.html
18. Horowitz, David. *Barack Obama's Rules for Revolution: the Alinsky Model*, Sherman Oaks, CA, 2009, 3-12.
19. ibid.
20. ibid, p.22
21. http://www.biblein90days.org/en/quotes/search.asp?category=Presidents+and+the+Bible
22. ibid
23. ibid
24. http://www.whatchristianswanttoknow.com/quotes-about-the-bible-25-awesome-sayings/
25. http://www.truthfulwords.org/articles/whyread.html
26. http://www.turnbacktogod.com/bible-quotes-from-famous-people/
27. http://www.biblein90days.org/en/quotes/search.asp?category=Presidents+and+the+Bible
28. http://www.inspirationalstories.com/1/106.html http://georgewashingtoninn.wordpress.com/2009/03/21/the-legend-of-the-cherry-tree/
29. Katsh, Abraham. *The Biblical Heritage of American Democracy*, New York, 1977: 97.
30. http://www.themoralliberal.com/2012/10/13/oct-13-advice-to-america-from-the-iron-lady/
31. ibid
32. "Livni Tells Kerry: Conflict is Becoming Religious", Israel National News, March 1, 2010.

CHAPTER SEVEN

1. http://jpetrie.myweb.uga.edu/poor_richard.html
2. http://en.wikipedia.org/wiki/Arab_Spring
3. http://littlegreenfootballs.com/article/40675_Romney_in_Israel-_Palestinian_Culture_Is_Inferior

4. http://www.frc.org/issueanalysis/islam-shariah-law-and-the-american-constitution
5. http://www.cnn.com/2012/03/08/world/meast/israel-iran-relations/index.html
6. http://en.wikipedia.org/wiki/Iranian_Revolution
7. http://en.wikipedia.org/wiki/Iran_hostage_crisis
8. February 11, 1979 (according to Dilip Hiro in The Longest War p.32) p.108 from Excerpts from Speeches and Messages of Imam Khomeini on the Unity of the Muslims.
9. http://www.nationalreview.com/articles/227772/fall-shah/peter-w-rodman
10. "U.S. Intelligence Unsure Over the Muslim Brotherhood", Jerusalem Post, February 17, 2011.
11. http://www.youtube.com/watch?v=-jq8bfKWTKA
12. http://www.cbn.com/cbnnews/insideisrael/2011/January/What-is-the-Muslim-Brotherhood-/
13. ibid
14. http://www.discoverthenetworks.org/guideDesc.asp?catid=8&type=group
15. http://www.pewglobal.org/2010/12/02/muslims-around-the-world-divided-on-hamas-and-hezbollah/
16. http://www.examiner.com/article/president-obama-the-egyptian-people-have-inspired-us-and-changed-the-world
17. http://www.revolutionary-war-and-beyond.com/john-adams-quotes-3.html
18. http://edition.cnn.com/2012/09/11/world/meast/egpyt-us-embassy-protests/index.html
19. http://en.wikipedia.org/wiki/Libyan_civil_war
    http://en.wikipedia.org/wiki/2011_military_intervention_in_Libya
20. http://www.state.gov/secretary/rm/2011/10/175999.htm
21. http://www.examiner.com/article/bbc-report-libyan-rebels-to-establish-sharia-law
    http://www.cnn.com/2011/10/26/world/africa/libya-sharia/index.html
22. http://news.yahoo.com/blogs/envoy/menacing-libyan-crowd-forces-returned-libyan-jew-flee-174235036.html
    http://www.npr.org/2011/10/03/141014576/hostile-crowd-forces-libyan-jew-out-of-synagogue

23. http://www.politico.com/news/stories/0912/81091.html
24. http://www.breitbart.com/Breitbart-TV/2012/09/13/Clinton-Mohammed-Video-Disgusting
25. http://abcnews.go.com/blogs/politics/2012/09/ambassador-susan-rice-libya-attack-not-premeditated
26. http://www.barenakedislam.com/2012/10/12/egypt-now-allows-sharia-sanctioned-abductions-and-forced-conversions-of-young-christian-girls-to-islam
    http://womenagainstshariah.blogspot.com/2012/08/egypt-christians-threatened-for-selling.html
    http://shariaunveiled.wordpress.com/2012/09/29/exodus-christians-flee-egypt-after-muslim-death-threats
27. http://www.memritv.org/clip/en/3702.htm
28. http://readersupportednews.org/opinion2/266-32/5421-kucinich-nato-war-still-a-bad-deal
29. http://www.bbc.co.uk/news/world-africa-14603245
30. http://www.thenational.ae/news/world/middle-east/fears-of-islamists-taking-over-syria-fuelling-moscows-support-for-damascus
31. http://www.israelnationalnews.com/News/News.aspx/163579
32. http://www.nydailynews.com/opinion/hatred-jews-article-1.1184968#ixzz29l9eMjIx
33. http://www.israelnationalnews.com/News/News.aspx/161145

CHAPTER EIGHT

1. http://www.think-israel.org/chweidan.3000yrsovereignty.html
2. http://israelseen.com/2011/01/05/the-settlements-issue-distorting-the-geneva-convention-and-the-oslo-accords/
3. ibid
4. http://en.wikipedia.org/wiki/Levy_Report
5. http://elderofziyon.blogspot.co.il/2012/07/english-translation-of-legal-arguments.html
6. http://www.israelnationalnews.com/News/News.aspx/163790
7. http://en.wikipedia.org/wiki/Palestinian_refugee
8. ibid
9. ibid

10. http://en.wikipedia.org/wiki/
   Jewish_exodus_from_Arab_and_Muslim_countries
11. http://honestreporting.com/hudna-with-hamas
12. ibid
13. http://www.goodreads.com/quotes/5543-insanity-is-doing-the-
   same-thing-over-and-over-again
14. http://www.nti.org/gsn/article/israeli-defenses-not-ready-missile-
   onslaught-lawmaker-says
15. http://www.youtube.com/watch?v=_VXXwyl5G0A
16. ibid

CHAPTER NINE

1. http://www.mefacts.com/cached.asp?x_id=11024
2. http://finance.fortune.cnn.com/2012/01/25/eric-klinenberg-going-
   solo
3. http://www.jpost.com/Opinion/Op-EdContributors/Article.
   aspx?id=70595
4. http://www.theettingerreport.com/Demographic-Scare.
   aspx?page=4
5. http://www.israelhayom.com/site/newsletter_opinion.php?id=569
6. http://www.theettingerreport.com/Print.
   aspx?printpath=%2FOpEd%2FOpEd---Israel-
   Hayom%2FDemographic-Optimism-upon-the-Jewish-New-Year-
   (Sep
7. http://www.jpost.com/Opinion/Op-EdContributors/Article.
   aspx?id=70595
8. http://www.israelnationalnews.com/News/News.aspx/151737
9. http://www.israelhayom.com/site/newsletter_opinion.php?id=569
10. ibid.
11. http://en.wikiquote.org/wiki/David_Ben-Gurion
12. http://en.wikipedia.org/wiki/Operation_Opera
13. http://www.israelnationalnews.com/News/News.aspx/144385
14. http://www.jewishvirtuallibrary.org/jsource/US-Israel/intell_coop.
   html
15. Rubin, David. *The Islamic Tsunami: Israel and America in the Age
   of Obama*, Shiloh Israel Press: Jerusalem, 2010.
16. http://www.familysecuritymatters.org/publications/detail/
   exclusive-why-is-american-birth-rate-declining

CHAPTER TEN

1. http://www.britannia.com/history/docs/peacetime.html
2. http://www.bobdylan.com/us/songs/neighborhood-bully
3. http://rt.com/news/morsi-gaza-israel-agression-160/
4. http://online.wsj.com/article/SB100014241278873233532045781 28880612421650.html
5. http://en.wikipedia.org/wiki/Israeli_Air_Force
6. http://www.jpost.com/DiplomacyAndPolitics/Article. aspx?id=293230
7. http://en.wikiquote.org/wiki/David_Ben-Gurion
8. http://forward.com/articles/131135/why-some-jewish-stars-support-israeli-artistic-boy/#
9. http://www.thejewishweek.com/news/breaking_news/mandy_ patinkin_backs_actor_boycott_settlements_during_israel_trip
10. http://www.sichosinenglish.org/books/when-silence-is-a-sin/16. htm
11. http://en.wikipedia.org/wiki/Balfour_Declaration

BACK COVER

1. http://abcnews.go.com/WNT/video/netanyahu-palestinians-recognize-jewish-state-14594675
2. http://www.ynetnews.com/articles/0,7340,L-3707501,00.html
3. http://www.jihadwatch.org/2012/10/hamas-top-dog-khaled-mashaal-nothing-will-restore-the-homeland-but-jihad-the-rifle-and-self-sacrific.html

Other Books By David Rubin

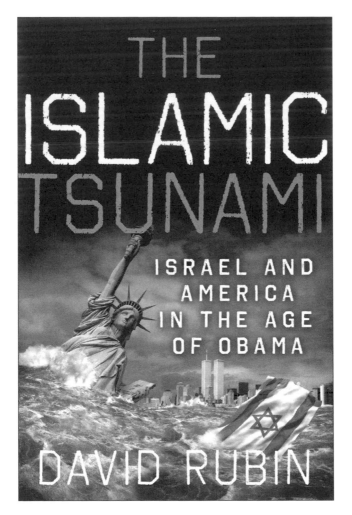

The Islamic Tsunami
Israel And America In The Age Of Obama
ISBN: 978-0-9829067-0-5

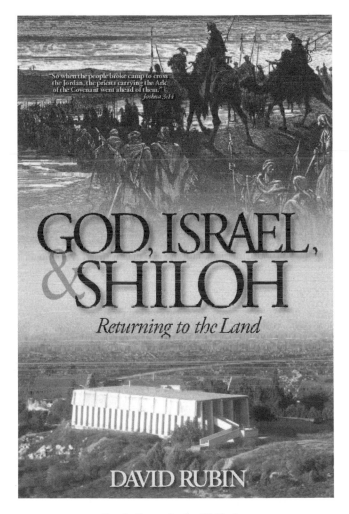

God, Israel, & Shiloh
Returning To The Land
ISBN: 978-0-9829067-2-9